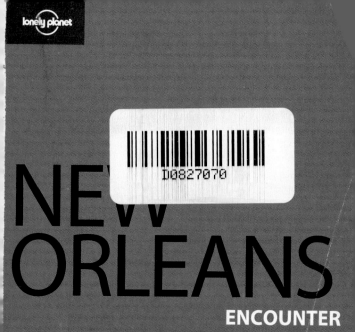

lonely planet

NEW
ORLEANS

ENCOUNTER

ADAM KARLIN

New Orleans Encounter

Published by Lonely Planet Publications Pty Ltd
ABN 36 005 607 983

Australia	Head Office, Locked Bag 1, Footscray, Vic 3011
	☎ 03 8379 8000 fax 03 8379 8111
	talk2us@lonelyplanet.com.au
USA	150 Linden St, Oakland, CA 94607
	☎ 510 250 6400
	toll free 800 275 8555
	fax 510 893 8572
	info@lonelyplanet.com
UK	2nd fl, 186 City Rd
	London EC1V 2NT
	☎ 020 7106 2100 fax 020 7106 2101
	go@lonelyplanet.co.uk

This title was commissioned in Lonely Planet's Oakland office and produced by: **Commissioning Editor** Jennye Garibaldi **Coordinating Editor** Maryanne Netto **Coordinating Cartographer** Andy Rojas **Layout Designer** Jacqui Saunders **Assisting Editors** Susie Ashworth, Kristin Odijk **Managing Editors** Sasha Baskett, Katie Lynch **Managing Cartographer** Alison Lyall **Cover Image Research** provided by lonelyplanetimages.com **Project Manager** Eoin Dunlevy **Managing Layout Designer** Sally Darmody **Thanks to** Nigel Chin, Nick Colicchia, Joshua Geoghegan, Jim Hsu, Chris Lee Ack, Wayne Murphy, Malisa Plesa, Michael Ruff

ISBN 978 1 74059 557 5

Printed through Colorcraft Ltd, Hong Kong.
Printed in China.

Acknowledgement: Transit map © 2009 New Orleans Regional Transit Authority. Map by Craig Dies, Let's Bus it. www.letsbusit.com.

HOW TO USE THIS BOOK
Colour-Coding & Maps

Colour-coding is used for symbols on maps and in the text that they relate to (eg all eating venues on the maps and in the text are given a green knife and fork symbol). Each neighborhood also gets its own colour, and this is used down the edge of the page and throughout that neighborhood section.

Shaded yellow areas on the maps denote 'areas of interest' – for their historical significance, their attractive architecture or their great bars and restaurants. We encourage you to head to these areas and just start exploring!

Send us your feedback We love to hear from readers – your comments help make our books better. We read every word you send us, and we always guarantee that your feedback goes straight to the appropriate authors. The most useful submissions are rewarded with a free book. To send us your updates and find out about Lonely Planet events, newsletters and travel news visit our award-winning website: *lonelyplanet.com/contact*.

Note: We may edit, reproduce and incorporate your comments in Lonely Planet products such as guidebooks, websites and digital products, so let us know if you don't want your comments reproduced or your name acknowledged. For a copy of our privacy policy visit *lonelyplanet.com/privacy*.

ADAM KARLIN

On Adam's first trip to New Orleans, as a college freshman, he was *that* guy: the Bourbon St boozer who never leaves the French Quarter. To make up for this grievous error, for this book he threw himself into the Crescent City and its cast of chefs, bartenders, waiters, social workers, community organizers, lawyers, beer brewers, journalists, musicians, artists and every other funky thread of the New Orleans tapestry. New Orleans has struck Adam, an itinerant wanderer, as a city that could be home. And that's the highest compliment he could give any place he's written on for Lonely Planet.

ADAM'S THANKS

Thanks: Randy for the tour, Diana and John for the pad, David for being my first friend, Wil for showing off his city, Allison for help with the intro, Zach and Ted for their perspective, Andy for giving me a place to crash, Sean F for discovering the city with me, Shane for fresh eyes, Noah for offering to sweep out my car and being a generally stand-up guy, Lisa and Sean M for their help, mom and dad for the usual, Jennye for being a patient and excellent editor and New Orleans for being what it is.

Cover photograph Man playing a trumpet in the French Quarter, Bob Krist/Corbis. **Internal photographs** p56, p69, p79, p105 by Adam Karlin; p25 Andy Levin/Alamy; p26 James Davis Photography/Alamy; p58 Jeffrey Anding; p60 Travel Division Images/Alamy; p106 Webstream/Alamy; p132 Jim West/Alamy; p137 Wallace Weeks/Alamy. All other photographs by Lonely Planet Images, and by Jerry Alexander p15, p93, p119, p120; Olivier Cirendini p126; Richard Cummins p4, p6 (bottom), p8, p13, p18, p20, p21, p30 (top left & bottom), p33, p34, p39, p63, p104, p112, p125, p128, p136, p139; Jon Davison p42, p134; John Elk III p29, p48, p122; Lee Foster p6 (top), p140; Rick Gerharter p138; Lou Jones p123; Ray Laskowitz p11, p16, p19, p22, p23, p30 (top right), p45, p46, p66, p78, p80, p87, p95, p116, p124, p127, p130; Margie Politzer p101, p110; Neil Setchfield p141.

All images are copyright of the photographers unless otherwise indicated. Many of the images in this guide are available for licensing from **Lonely Planet Images**: www.lonelyplanetimages.com.

St Charles Ave streetcar

CONTENTS

THIS IS NEW ORLEANS

There are two views on this town post-Hurricane Katrina. One: New Orleans is back. Two: New Orleans is still suffering. And there's the truth, which lies somewhere between these opinions.

Sweet zydeco music like a bug's buzz on Bayou St John and bacon cooked in brown sugar in the Bywater; a second line dancing up Esplanade after church on Sunday; the wind bending the trees in the Garden District while folks kick back with a beer and a boil (of crawfish). Welcome home, New Orleans.

Milneburg houses tagged with rescue-worker code listing the number of dead within; suburban split-levels in Lakeview whose owners never returned; stretches of the Lower Ninth Ward that aren't devastated so much as turned into wilderness, reclaimed by nature. Where is home, New Orleans?

Being made. New Orleans is neither back nor gone: she's changed, simultaneously one of the oldest cities in the country and the newest, a child of America who acknowledges both the troubles of her history and the fact those growing pains give her the nation's most distinctive sense of place. And she's passionately embracing the future, with every green building project and community organization and arts center and sustainable business that crops up. These places serve both the home that was and the home that will be: the new New Orleans, not so much reborn, as reincarnated.

The character of the city and the home she's rebuilding is partly in the hands of travelers, backbone of the local economy. But don't push her too hard. New Orleans doesn't do things like the rest of America. She cares less about deadlines and more about taking time for a neighbor, planting strong trees that withstand salt water and giving *lagniappe*, Creole for 'a little extra.'

So hold tight, ya' heard? She *is* coming back. And in New Orleans the wait is always worth it.

Top The city skyline looms on a ferry ride (p155) across the water **Bottom** Dining out on good food and balcony views in the historic French Quarter (p46)

>HIGHLIGHTS

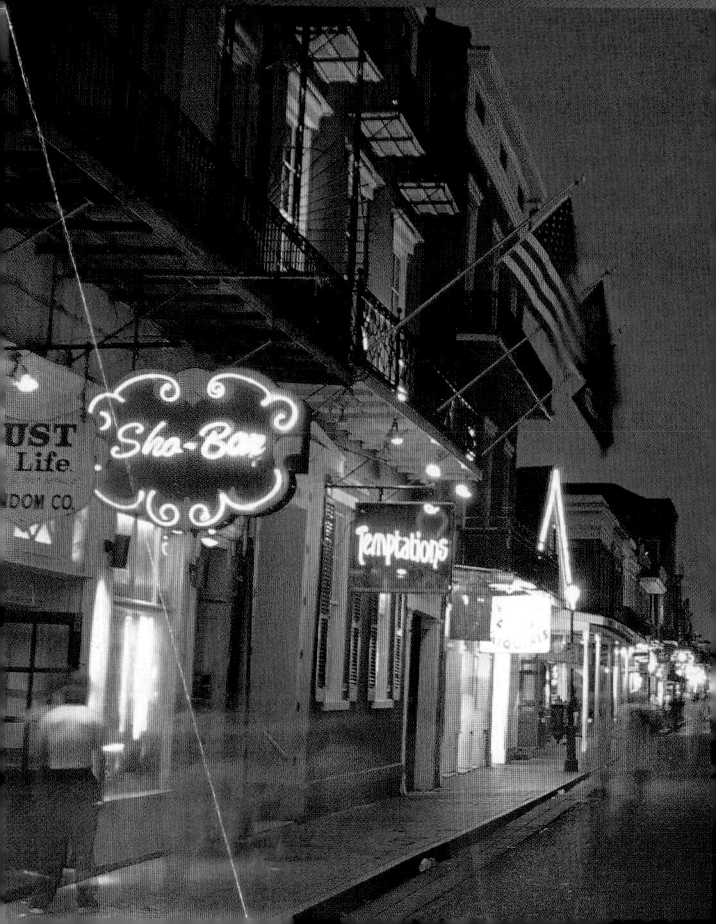

Bourbon St alight in the quiet of the night

>1 MARDI GRAS

GET YOUR PARTY ON AT MARDI GRAS

Play the word association game and 'New Orleans' and 'Mardi Gras'
end up going together like peanut butter and jelly – or, as is more
likely in this town, a beer and a shot.

That connection makes sense, although maybe not in the way
you imagine. Yes, Mardi Gras is the ultimate expression of the New
Orleans love of life, and in those lines of paraders and revelers is
more than an embrace of hedonism. Mardi Gras contains within its
pageantry much of the history, social divisions, community connections and cultural background of this town.

To begin with, Mardi Gras is rooted in the Catholic tradition of
allowing an annual period of profanity, in the original Latin sense of
the word 'Pro fane,' to come (and act as you please) before the temple. This was the day sin could be let loose, desires embraced and
the inner animal indulged before the period of Lent and the human
discipline required for fasting (hence also 'carnival' from the Italian
carne levare – to remove meat). This link to Catholic character is quintessentially New Orleanian, a phenomenon explored in museums
like the Presbytère (p43), dedicated to the history of Mardi Gras and,
ironically, housed in a former residence of Capuchin monks.

But these French-Spanish Catholic roots (for New Orleans was originally a French-Spanish Catholic town) were supplanted and altered by
the arrival of American immigrants after the Louisiana Purchase. The
Americans wanted to prove their wealth, embrace a new culture and
build their own social conventions. So they formed krewes, the parad-
ing societies of Mardi Gras that sometimes celebrate, sometimes
subvert and sometimes act as the city's aristocracy, with names that
literally evoke myth and kingship: Momus, Comus, Hermes and Rex.
And New Orleanians bow to this monarchy, literally baring themselves (to the infamous Mardi Gras catcall: 'Show your tits!') for the
chance of being tossed plastic beads from royalty on a float. You can
see some of the best floats, by the way, at Mardi Gras World (p67).

Yet Mardi Gras also became a means for blacks to assert their traditions, even co-opt power. Hence the ceding of some parts of the city
to the famous Mardi Gras Indians, African Americans who dress like

the Native Americans who fought against white invaders; the Skull and Bones clubs, who evoke death to oppose the celebration of life; the Baby Dolls, black women who reclaim their womanhood while playing the part of an ingénue; and 'super krewes,' like Bacchus, who epitomize America by allowing anyone who can pay the dues to join their club. Visit the Backstreet Cultural Museum (p101) and The House of Dance and Feathers (p55) to connect to these multiple cultures at the heart of many New Orleanian communities.

>2 MUSIC

LIVE LIVE MUSIC

Live music is not just the core of the New Orleans nightlife scene. It's a keystone of this city's character. And a huge gift the Crescent City has given the world.

For hundreds of years African American slaves in the USA were denied the right to congregate, celebrate, speak their old languages or engage in their old rituals, but for almost a century New Orleans was not America. Under French law slaves could gather once a week, in Congo Sq (p144), and recall the rituals of West Africa. They kept a musical tradition alive, and in a sense, that tradition kept slaves alive.

Music was not just something to listen to: it was the soul of a people displaced. In parts of town settled by the French (or American areas mimicking the French), knowledge of classical music was a sign, by continental European values, of a healthy education. Black and white worlds met when white men kept black women as official mistresses under a system known as *placage* (see p144). While never officially married, the white male was expected to handsomely house and provide for his mistress and any resulting children. These mixed-race progeny were often educated in Europe. The music of these three worlds met on the Mississippi and gave us jazz and the foundation of all American pop. Music was the voice of New Orleans.

And still is. Let us be clear: good gigs pop off *every* night here (p32). New Orleanians go out to dance and drink, yes, but by and large they want to do so to the accompaniment of some great tunes. Maybe it's punk at the Saturn Bar (p61). Nah? A brass band at the Maple Leaf (p99) or Le Bon Temps Roulé (p98) then; you haven't heard Outkast till you've heard them covered by a tuba, trombone and trumpet ensemble. Indie rock? Roll to the Circle Bar (p71) or the Saint (p84) and rock it out with Tulane law students and folks sporting more ink than a newspaper plant. Now, we must be missing some genre of tunes…oh yeah, jazz. Just, you know, the soul of the damn city. Dude: just wander up Frenchmen St (p61) and follow your ears wherever they find happiness. You'll likely be pulled in several dozen directions, all of them leading to a happy gig-grounded ending.

>3 FOOD

EAT 'TIL YOU DIE

This author is typing these words in New Orleans. That means he just ate better than you.

This is, after all, New *Orleans*, a city founded by those gastronomic pioneers: the French, who never met a strange ingredient they couldn't craft into a work of culinary art. And my oh my, how the local ingredients must have seemed strange and new and terrifying. Mud bugs and lizards and things that any proper human would step on rather than fry.

But wait. Frying that ugly-looking critter makes it taste *so good*. And the Native Americans who lived here already knew that contrary to its appearance (hostile swamp), south Louisiana is like heaven's own grocery store, stocked with some of the tastiest protein in nature. But early settlers had to deal with lots of diseases and disasters, too. A cosmopolitan mix of immigrants (dominated by the food-mad French) combined with good ingredients and the possibility of death by yellow fever caused New Orleanians to develop a unique cuisine. It's unapologetically rich – largely because the orginal chefs figured they should eat, drink and make as merry as possible since tomorrow they could well be dead.

The tradition continues. If you make friends with local chefs (very easy, by the way, as this city attracts plenty of young knives), their invite to you often takes this form: 'Come over for dinner. I will *kill* you.' There is no such thing as moderation in New Orleans: it's excess, excess, excess, from praline bacon at Elizabeth's (p58) – yeah you right, to pig cracklin' with cane syrup at Cochon (p70) – *yeah* you right, to alligator sausage cheesecake at Jaques-Imo's (p96) – *yeah* you *right*, to peanut butter bacon burgers at Yo Mama's (p49) – Jesus.

Want to go high end? New Orleans does high-end gourmet, but gourmet of the old-school type that serves the king a fatted pig and melts some foie gras on it, too. There's the divine duck-fat-fried chicken and waffles in Mat & Naddies (p96), garlicky Parmesan cheese fries finished with Krispy Kreme bread pudding at Boucherie (p92); and oysters glinting like little gastronomic orgasms on a shucker's knife in Casamento's (p93). Yes, our language got a little sexual

there. But eating well is all about losing your inhibitions, and that's what New Orleans is about. That term used above, 'Yeah you right,' is something of the city's motto. It means 'yes,' in one way. But is also means, 'Do it. Screw it. The hell with the consequences.' Learn it, live it, be a New Orleanian.

>4 BARS

THE BEST BAR SCENE IN AMERICA

New Orleans is a city that lives life to the hilt. Sensory pleasures aren't just important; they're a crucial component of life, and one way of training your senses is by heightening and then destroying them via long nights out on the town.

That said, we need to wean you off the idea New Orleans is all about Bourbon St. Bourbon is where tourists go to unleash the repressed id of the American psyche. If you have no concept of kissing life full on the lips, the first few times you do smooch existence will be messy (as Bourbon invariably is). But being a New Orleanian means constantly kissing life, and folks here practice in the city's excellent bars.

The best ones manage to combine camaraderie, community, good layout and even sophistication. New York and San Francisco can crow all they want; bartenders here are often *really* good at mixing drinks, and they rarely if ever have attitude. Take Cure (p98) and Tonique (p49), where the cocktails are as elegant as the interior of a china shop and as strong as the bull that's about to wreck it (and you). Both bars also have great outdoor gardens, which is a crucial component of any good New Orleans drinking establishment.

The neighborhood bar that's friendly enough to be a dive, cool enough to be a lounge, and too original and scruffy to be either is the epitome of the New Orleans drinking venue. Take, for a small sample, St Joe's (p99) and its mojitos; Mid-City Yacht Club (p111), built literally from the surrounding neighborhood via hurricane debris; Molly's at the Market (p49) and its resident cat, frozen Irish coffee and urn containing the ashes of its founder; and Mimi's in the Marigny (p59), home of the two 'TPs': tatted punks and tapas plates. All of the above aren't just great bars (although they are that), they're the cornerstones of their respective neighborhoods as well.

There are plenty of straight-up sleazy, greasy, glorious dives if such is your poison. If you need to drink till the cold, cruel light of dawn shatters your sanity, by all means hit up such lovely establishments like Snake & Jake's (p98) and Ms Mae's (p98).

BAR OR CLUB? LIVE OR DIVE?

Many bars in New Orleans double as live music venues, and many of the city's best gig venues play the part of bar for several days in the week. This city is too musically in-clined to suffer rigid distinctions between the genres. We haven't divided our reviews between bars and live music clubs, since one spot so often ends up wearing both hats. But we have tried to identify what goes on — booze or music or both. However, there is a clear delineation between bars, dives, lounges etc. Dives are grungy, grotty and lovable; bars can run from neighborhood pub to sleek hotel hotspot; and lounges are the most posh of the scene.

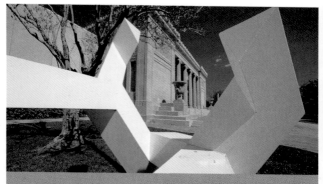

>5 MUSEUMS

MORE THAN JUST A MUSEUM

Most visitors don't think of New Orleans as a city of museums, but this town embraces its intellectual pursuits with the passion it reserves for a good meal and music. And its museums are not just institutions of learning; they're often archives of one of the richest, most distinct cultures in an America where local character can often be swallowed by big-box blandness.

Take, for example, the Backstreet Cultural Museum (p101) and the House of Dance and Feathers (p55), both specifically dedicated to the African American New Orleanian experience, its historical roots and cultural growth. What could seem like houses of 'stuff' becomes a discussion, living and breathing, with the neighborhoods that are the backbone of New Orleans. Just as fascinating are the Cabildo (p39) and the Historic New Orleans Collection (p39), which dig deep under the city's skin in the more traditional way of museums – with painstaking and intimate historical detail.

If art is your thing, the New Orleans Museum of Art (p106), pictured above, is the crown jewel in the city's collection, but don't pass up institutions like the Ogden (p67), which hosts Thursday concerts where you can a) listen to music, b) peruse paintings and c) drink. What could be more New Orleans?

>6 SHOPPING

MEANDERING ALONG MAGAZINE STREET

Magazine St is the cute heart of New Orleans fashion. It's full of shopping stores and yuppie goodies, but it never feels pretentious or stuck up: just a place where folks who need retail therapy will find it. The variety of goods available for purchase is varied, running from summer shoes to ousider art.

Speaking of the latter, if you start out in the Lower Garden District you'll pass by Simon of New Orleans (p80) and its racks of antiques and hand-painted signs, ubiquitous throughout the city. Aidan Gill (p78), with its rows of cufflinks and shaving goodness, will keep men happy while the women go for undergarment glamour in Trashy Diva (p80). Unisex vintage shopping is the name of the game at Funky Monkey (p78).

Further along, in Uptown there are all sorts of stores selling the swish summer dresses beloved of the New Orleans female: cloyingly cute Sweet Pea and Tulip (p92) springs to mind. But you can't leave New Orleans without at least one ironic inside-joke T-shirt from the designers at Dirty Coast (p91); if someone gives you a fist bump for your 504: Soul is Waterproof tee, you'll know they've also been on a Magazine meander.

>7 GREEN SPACES

AUDUBON PARK AND TULANE ON A SUNNY DAY

New Orleans is a great place for green spaces, more fecund than any other American city we can imagine. A simple yet powerful way of experiencing this fertile phenomenon is strolling through Audubon Park and Tulane when the weather's fine and the leaves are lathered by sunshine into a pale-green transparency.

Audubon Park (p87) isn't just a lovely place for a walk; here you'll find the city's excellent zoo, sweet little snowball stands and, along the perimeters of the park, some of the city's most beautiful homes. Couples kiss, dogs chase Frisbees, children run barefoot and all is basically well with the universe.

Just north of here is Tulane University (p90); whether you love its student body or not (for the record, that opinion divides much of the city), few folks would say anything that detracts from Tulane's lovely campus. Watch students engage in rigorous intellectual pursuit (or get ready for the weekend kegger); and if you feel the need to relive some *Animal House* days, join them for a beer or 12 at the Boot (p97).

>8 GALLERIES

ARTS AMBLING IN THE WAREHOUSE DISTRICT

Following the lead of many American cities, New Orleans has revital-
ized its once-dodgy urban core, creating an arts district and studio
spaces out of a series of warehouses. See www.neworleansartsdistrict
.com for details.

Head down Julia St if you're here on the first Saturday of the
month, when the city's many galleries have an open house and street
parties are the name of the game. But don't fret if you can't make the
stroll; all of the galleries here will happily give you a look around as
long as you make arrangements a little in advance. Artists like Jean
Bragg (p68) are masters of capturing nostalgia in New Orleans in an
elegiac way, and painting new tropes on a city rediscovering its identity. To expand on this theme of remembering and re-creating New
Orleans, make sure you pop into the Preservation Resource Center
(p67), where you can learn about the city's neighborhoods and their
historic buildings in incredible detail; and the Contemporary Arts
Center (p66), where new creativity is given soaring life in a grand
warehouse space.

>9 SECRET SPOTS

ROUGH DIAMONDS REVEALED

New Orleans has her hard edges. But in between the grit is the spirit of a city that's as resilient, and beautiful, as the marsh that surrounds her. You won't often find tourists at the following spots. You will find something like the soul of this great city.

Check out KKProjects (p54), one of the most innovative arts spaces we can imagine, which works to break up the hard edge of the 'hood with gardens and public arts projects. Just down the way, Kermit Ruffins leads some of the best live music in New Orleans every Thursday night in scruffy little Vaughan's (p61). Where did Barack Obama eat when he came to New Orleans? In a little restaurant in a little house run by a little woman (Leah Chase, above) with a soul like steel: Dooky Chase, civil rights hangout and presidential nosh pit (p108). Just around the way is the James Beard–award-winning famous fried chicken of Miss Willie Mae Seaton (p110). You wouldn't expect a free bluegrass concert to rock the Hi Ho Lounge (p59), but here it is, every Monday, on dodgy St Claude Ave. And where else would we eat but with the at-risk youth cooking and prepping meals that are rebuilding New Orleans one plate of red beans at a time, in Café Reconcile (p81).

>NEW ORLEANS CALENDAR

And this month we have: party in the French Quarter. And next month? Party along Canal St. And there'll be parties along Bayou St John and concerts and crawfish boils and concerts and readings and concerts and literary festivals and concerts and open house days and concerts and concerts and concerts.

Lots of New Orleans events highlight the communities that make up this city – their traditions, food, history and, of course, tunes. Take those disparate notes, string them together over the course of 12 months and there's your New Orleans calendar: a year-long song for the city.

Beaded glory: a reveler at Mardi Gras (p10)

JANUARY

Sugar Bowl

☎ 828-2440; Superdome, 1500 Sugar Bowl Dr

This NCAA game between two of the nation's top-ranking college football teams takes place on New Year's Day in the downtown Superdome.

Battle of New Orleans Celebration

☎ 589-4428

On the weekend closest to January 8, volunteers stage a re-creation of the last great battle of the War of 1812 in Chalmette National Historical Park.

FEBRUARY

Mardi Gras Parades

St Charles Ave & Canal St

The greatest free show on earth gets going during the three weeks before Mardi Gras, culminating in multiple parades each day. Routes vary, but the largest krewes stage massive parades that run along sections of St Charles Ave and Canal St.

MARCH

St Patrick's Day

On March 17, watch parades depart from Molly's at the Market (p49) and Parasol's (p82).

Indian Sunday

www.mardigrasindians.com

On March 19, African Americans dressed as Indians parade through the heart of Mid-City.

Tennessee Williams Literary Festival

☎ 581-1144; www.tennesseewilliams .net

Four-day fête at the end of March, including a 'Stell-a-a-a!' shouting contest.

APRIL

French Quarter Festival

☎ 522-5730; www.fqfi.org

French Quarter Fest, held during the second or third weekend of April, celebrates superb music and scrumptious food.

Jazz Fest

www.nojazzfest.com

The Fair Grounds Race Track reverberates with good sounds, food, beer and crafts, over two weekends in late April and early May.

MAY

Wine & Food Experience

☎ 529-9463; www.nowfe.com

Well, this is just an excuse to act all highbrow, in the company of strangers, but it's fun if you like wine and food. And who in

New Orleans doesn't? You sign on (and pay a pretty penny) for various plans. 'Experiences' may include a vintner dinner, with wine-and-food pairings being the primary focus; an evening street fair on Royal St, made jolly by wine and song; and a whole host of tastings, seminars and brunches. Held in late May.

JUNE

Great French Market Creole Tomato Festival

☎ 636-1020; www.frenchquarter.com/events

Whether you say 'to-may-toe' or 'to-mah-toe,' you're pretty sure to dig this

Creole Tomato Festival parade at the French Market (p39)

celebration of the delta-bred red natives. If you're quickly tomatoed out, there's plenty of food and entertainment. Takes place in the French Market (p39) during the second weekend of the month.

JULY

Independence Day

On July 4, food stalls and stages set up on the riverfront, and spectacular fireworks light the sky over the 'Old Man' – the Mississippi River to celebrate American independence.

Essence Music Festival

☎ 800-274-9398; www.essence.com/essence/emf

Essence magazine sponsors a lineup of R&B, hip-hop and jazz and blues performances at the Superdome on the weekend closest to July 4; features big-name recording artists.

New Orleans' black community celebrate the red, white and blue on Independence Day

FINDING YOUR FARMER'S MARKET

New Orleans makes up for a lack of supermarkets with a surfeit of farmer's markets held at regular times throughout the year. Here's a list of some of our favorites:

Crescent City Farmer's Market Magazine St (700 Magazine St; ☼ 8am-noon Sat); Broad St (200 Broad St; ☼ 9am-1pm Tue)

German Coast Farmer's Market East Bank (Ormond Plantation, 13786 River Rd, Destrehan; ☼ 8am-noon Wed); West Bank (13969 River Rd, Lulin; ☼ 3-7pm Wed)

Gretna Farmer's Market (Huey P Long Ave, btwn Third & Fourth Sts, Gretna; ☼ 8:30am-12:30pm Sat)

Harrison Avenue Marketplace (801 Harrison Ave; ☼ 5-8pm every 2nd Sat)

Mid-City Green Market (3700 Orleans Ave; ☼ 3-7pm Thu)

Upper Ninth Ward Market (cnr St Claude Ave & Gallier St; ☼ 1-4pm Sat)

AUGUST

Satchmo SummerFest

☎ 636-1020; www.fqfi.org/satchmo summerfest

Louis Armstrong's birthday, August 4, is celebrated with four days of music and food in the French Quarter. Three stages present local talents in 'trad' jazz, contemporary jazz and brass bands. Throughout the fest, seminars at night are conducted by jazz writers for serious music fans.

SEPTEMBER

Southern Decadence

☎ 522-8057; www.southerndecadence .com

Billing itself the 'Gay Mardi Gras,' this five-day festival, held on Labor Day weekend, showcases music, food, street dancing and a Sunday parade that's everything you'd expect

from a city with a vital gay community and a rich history of masking and cross-dressing.

OCTOBER

Voodoo Music Experience

www.voodoomusicfest.com

Rock and roll tends to get overlooked in New Orleans, but not during Halloween weekend, when Voodoo Music Experience rocks City Park. Past acts have included the Foo Fighters, the Flaming Lips, Queens of the Stone Age, Billy Idol and Ryan Adams (all in one year!).

Halloween

Celebrated on October 31, Halloween is a holiday not taken lightly in New Orleans. Most of the fun is to be found in the giant costume party throughout the French Quarter. It's a big holiday for both local gays and tourists, with a lot of action centering on Bourbon St.

NOVEMBER

All Saints Day

On November 1, the city's cemeteries fill with people who pay their respects to ancestors and recently departed family and friends.

Bayou Bacchanal

www.bayoubacchanal.com

The first Saturday in November kicks off with New Orleans' Caribbean festival: steel drums, reggae and a big ol' parade on Canal St.

DECEMBER

Feux de Joie

☎ 524-0814

'Fires of joy' bonfires erupt along Mississippi River levees above Orleans Parish and below Baton Rouge on Christmas Eve (December 24). To reach the flames you must endure incredible traffic along narrow River Rd, or drop a pretty penny to see the fires from a riverboat.

The stately Cabildo (p39), doorway to Louisianan history

ITINERARIES

New Orleans is a city that rewards slow exploration, but sometimes folks get too locked into the syrupy pace of life down here and miss the Mardi Gras for the beads, as it were. Here we've included some guides to getting the most out of a Big Easy adventure.

DAY ONE

Listen up, class: before recess you're gonna learn a little something first. Get in the French Quarter and start your day in Jackson Sq (p42) amid the street artists and fortune tellers (prediction: you are about to have a lot of fun). Admire the St Louis Cathedral (p43), and visit the Cabildo (p39) and the Presbytère (p43) to ground yourself in the history of New Orleans and Mardi Gras.

Give yourself a lunch break at Coop's Place (p47) or Fiorella's (p47); the former serves Cajun and the latter Creole cuisine. Now pop in to see the Historic New Orleans Collection's (p39) inevitably excellent temporary exhibitions. Head to Louis Armstrong Park (p106), then drop by Congo Sq and the Backstreet Cultural Museum (p101) for grassroots displays on the city's street culture.

For dinner we recommend Bayona (p46) for a classically decadent, locally sourced four-star meal. Or, grab a half-pound burger at Port of Call (p48). Head to Frenchmen St and get your crawl on: catch some music at d.b.a (p61) or good drinks at R Bar (p60) – and drink some water before bed.

FORWARD PLANNING
Three weeks before you go Buy this book and see if any festivals are going down, and book tickets for any big-name shows you may want to see at Tipitina's (p99) or Le Petit Théâtre du Vieux Carré (p50).
One week before you go Try to organize a car rental. Make a booking at any of the high-end restaurants that catch your eye.
One day before you go Read the Gambit (www.bestofneworleans.com) and check www.nolafunguide.com to see what live music will be going on during your visit.

Top left Shark alert at the Aquarium of the Americas (p63) **Top right** Flamingos in the pink, Audubon Zoological Gardens (p87) **Bottom** A burst of azaleas in Louis Armstrong Park (p106)

V

ITINERARIES

DAY TWO

Time to explore two different sides of New Orleans.

Rent a car or hire a taxi and drive out to just north of the Bywater neighborhood to see KKProjects (p54) and Musicians' Village (p54), arts and housing projects that are the result of the community development constantly in operation behind the scenes. We'd also recommend driving into the nearby Lower Ninth Ward (p55) to witness firsthand how the community here is dealing with the disaster that was Hurricane Katrina. Grab lunch at Elizabeth's (p58) in a converted Bywater shack or hit the Joint (p59) for its excellent barbecue.

Now see some of New Orleans' prettiest, most manicured streets in the Garden and Lower Garden Districts. Take a drive down St Charles Ave or Prytania St and admire some of the most gorgeous mansions in the American south. Take some time to window-shop along Magazine St and have dinner at Mat & Naddie's (p96) in the Riverbend, before mojitos at St Joe's Bar (p99) in Uptown.

CHILD'S PLAY

This city is sort of like one giant playground for your wee ones. If you're looking to wear them out, start your day with some underwater adventures at the Aquarium of the Americas (p63). Following on, shrink the scope of your wildlife watching with a visit to the Insectarium (p66).

LIVIN' LA VIDA NOLA

If you've come to New Orleans to eat, drink and hear lots of good music, you can do so every night of the week. Many shows listed here come with good free (or cheap) food.

> Monday: Mark Braud Jazz Jam at Donna's Bar & Grill (p50) with red beans, rice and fried chicken; Bluegrass night at the Hi Ho Lounge (p59) with $1 red beans and rice.
> Tuesday: Rebirth Brass Band at Maple Leaf (p99), New Orleans Jazz Vipers at d.b.a. (p61).
> Wednesday: Tin Men with Washboard Chaz and Walter Wolfman Washington, both at d.b.a. (p61).
> Thursday: Kermit Ruffins at Vaughan's (p61) with free red beans and rice; Soul Rebels at Le Bon Temps Roule (p98).
> Friday: Joe Krown at Le Bon Temps Roule (p98), plus free oysters; Ellis Marsalis at Snug Harbor (p61).
> Saturday: John Boutté at d.b.a. (p61); DJ Soul Sister at Mimi's in the Marigny (p59).
> Sunday: Bruce Daigrepont and the Cajun Fais Do Do at Tipitina's (p99).

Horse statue cantering through the gates of Carousel Gardens (p101) at City Park

Let the little ones run wild in the Louisiana Children's Museum (p66) and go gaga for the floats, masks and parade paraphernalia at Mardi Gras World (p67). When the kids get hungry, give them a taste of local cuisine at colorful Joey K's (p81), then run across the street to look at Simon Hardeveld's funky signs (p80) or spook 'em (slightly) at Lafayette Cemetery (p75).

If they're not tuckered out, we recommend more close encounters with the animal world at the excellent Audubon Zoo (p87). And no child should visit New Orleans without getting the chance to romp through City Park (p104) and riding the carousel in Carousel Gardens & Storyland (p101).

New Orleans lit by night

NEIGHBORHOODS

This may seem like an odd observation, but bear with us. There are a lot of elements that make this city unique – Mardi Gras, Creole food, jazz music etc. But one of our favorite New Orleans qualities is the way the city can be crossed end to end without ever getting on the freeway.

That speaks of the fundamental principle of New Orleans urban planning: this city wasn't plotted, like so many American metropolises, by the whims of the driving class. It was laid out with residential needs in mind.

New Orleans feels like a city of interconnected neighborhoods rather than a series of exits off a concrete superstrip. And one of the losses caused by Hurricane Katrina was the erasure, or at least irrevocable change, wrought on several of the city's greatest neighborhoods.

Although the neighborhoods covered in this book are racially mixed, you may notice one demographic oddity: with the exception of the Tremé, these areas are whiter than the rest of town. The simple fact is that majority-black parts of New Orleans were disproportionately affected by the storm, and are still rebuilding.

The French Quarter – or Vieux Carré (Old Quarter), pronounced voo car-*ray* – was the original city, as planned by the French, an elegantly aged grid of shop fronts, iron lamps and courtyard gardens. North of here are the Creole faubourgs (neighborhoods) of the Marigny and the Bywater. This hip and occasionally edgy area marks the fall line between gentrification, artists' lofts and the poor periphery.

The Central Business District and Warehouse District encompass touristy sites and art galleries, while the Garden District, Lower Garden District and Uptown are a green, pleasantly yuppie stretch of shopping boutiques, beautiful houses and great restaurants. Where the Mississippi River bends is, well, Riverbend, essentially a student-filled extension of Uptown. Finally, Mid-City is exactly that: the middle ground of New Orleans, geographically, racially and economically. This area includes the Tremé, the nation's oldest African American neighborhood.

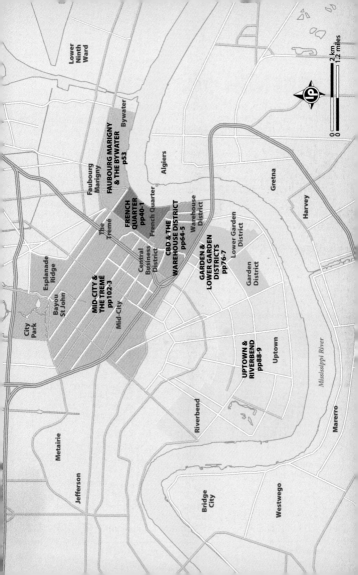

Lower
Ninth
Ward

Bywater

FAUBOURG MARIGNY
& THE BYWATER
p53

Faubourg
Marigny

Algiers

FRENCH
QUARTER
pp40-1

French Quarter

The Tremé

CBD & THE
WAREHOUSE DISTRICT
pp64-5

Warehouse
District

Central
Business
District

Gretna

Esplanade
Ridge

GARDEN &
LOWER GARDEN
DISTRICTS
pp76-7

Lower Garden
District

Harvey

Bayou
St John

MID-CITY &
THE TREMÉ
pp102-3

Garden
District

City
Park

Mid-City

Mississippi River

UPTOWN &
RIVERBEND
pp88-9

Marerro

Metairie

Uptown

Riverbend

Jefferson

Bridge
City

Westwego

2 km
1.2 miles
0
0

>FRENCH QUARTER

For many visitors, the French Quarter, along with some glimpses of downtown, and the road to the airport, *is* New Orleans. The Quarter is in some ways New Orleans magnified, and in some places (like Bourbon St) nothing like New Orleans. Some of the best French, Spanish and Creole architecture in the city is in its atmospheric alleyways fronting sweet-scented gardens. The Quarter may be over-marketed, but that's because this is New Orleans at her most accessible, from great restaurants to chaos-inducing bars to twee antique shops, all connected by an orderly grid of torch-lit pedestrian alleys. Incidentally, this *was* New Orleans, as designed by the French; Rampart St is named so because it marked where the ramparts (walls) of New Orleans once stood.

We'd advise you to explore outside this area, but by no means should you ignore it, either. Not that you could.

FRENCH QUARTER

👁 SEE
Cabildo 1 E3
French Market 2 F3
Historic New Orleans
   Collection 3 D4
Jackson Square 4 E3
New Orleans Pharmacy
   Museum 5 E4
Presbytère 6 E3
St Louis Cathedral 7 E3
Ursuline Convent 8 F2

🏠 SHOP
Boutique du Vampyre ...9 E3
Centuries 10 D4

Faulkner House
   Bookstore 11 E3
Hové Parfumeur 12 E3
Louisiana Music Factory ..13 D5
Maskarade 14 E3

🍴 EAT
Bayona 15 D3
Café du Monde 16 F3
Clover Grill 17 E2
Coop's Place 18 F2
Dickie Brennan's 19 C5
Fiorella's 20 F2
GW Fins 21 C4
Port of Call 22 F1
Yo Mama's 23 E3

🍸 DRINK
Carousel Bar 24 D5
French 75 ....25 C4
Molly's at the Market ..26 F2
Tonique 27 D2

⭐ PLAY
Donna's Bar & Grill 28 D2
Le Petit Théâtre du
   Vieux Carré 29 E3
One Eyed Jacks 30 E3
Preservation Hall 31 D3

Please see over for map

SEE

☎ CABILDO

☎ 568-6968; http://lsm.crt.state.la.us; 701 Chartres St; adult/concession/child under 12 $6/5/free; ⏱ 9am-5pm Tue-Sun

The former seat of government in colonial Louisiana now serves as the gateway to exploring the history of the state in general, and New Orleans in particular. It's also a magnificent building in its own right; the elegant Cabildo marries elements of Spanish colonial architecture and French urban design better than most buildings in the city. Exhibits range from Native American tools to wanted posters for escaped slaves to a gallery's worth of paintings of stone-faced old New Orleanians. This was the site of the Louisiana Purchase ceremonies, the city council hall of New Orleans up until the 1850s and courtroom for *Plessy v. Ferguson*, the 1896 landmark US Supreme Court case that legalized segregation under the 'separate but equal' doctrine. Give yourself at least two hours to explore.

☎ FRENCH MARKET

☎ 522-2623; www.frenchmarket.org; 1008 N Peters St

For centuries, this was the great bazaar and pulsing commercial heart of much of New Orleans, and even if it's a bit sanitized today, it's still great fun: a safari through a tourist jungle of curios, flea markets and shiny, harmless junk that all equals great family-friendly fun. Occasionally you will spot some genuinely fascinating and/or unique work of art or craft.

☎ HISTORIC NEW ORLEANS COLLECTION

☎ 523-4662; www.hnoc.org; 533 Royal St; admission free, guided tours $5, ⏱ Merieult House & Louisiana History Galleries 9:30am-4:30pm Tue-Sat, from 10:30am Sun, Williams Gallery 9:30am-4:30pm Tue-Sat, closed Sun

This combination of preserved buildings, museums and research centers is arguably the best short

History and art at the Cabildo

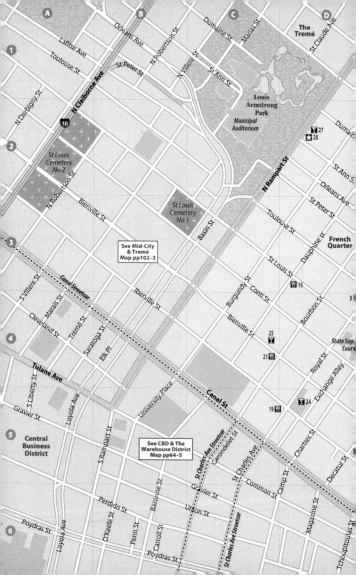

E   F   G   H

Faubourg Marigny

Faubourg
Marigny

Burgundy St
Esplanade Ave
Chartres St
22

Mandeville St

Margny St

Decatur St

Dauphine St

Barracks St

N Peters St

Ursulines Ave

Governor Nicholls St

Bourbon St

Elysian Fields Ave

Esplanade

hillip St

Royal St

Chartres St

Decatur St

French Market Place

N Peters St

8

18
20

26

17

2

Ursulines

12

Mississippi River

14

Lower Pontalba
Buildings

9

Antoine Alley

6

Pirate's Alley

7

Dumaine

11

4

New Orleans
Welcome Center

1

Jackson
Square

16

Decatur St

Moon Walk

29

Upper
Pontalba
Buildings

Wilkinson St

Jackson
Brewery

5

Toulouse

Riverfront Streetcar

Morgan St

Woldenberg
Park

Bienville

eters St

Algiers

N Front St

Clay St

Ferry to Algiers

Powder St

Convention
Centre Blvd

Canal

Canal St
Wharf

0   200 m
0   0.1 miles

introduction to the city's history on offer. The complex of historic buildings is anchored by **Merieult House** and a series of regularly rotating exhibits located in its 1st-floor **Williams Gallery**. Upstairs, in the Louisiana History Galleries, the meticulously researched **Merieult History Tour** is a dive into 11 galleries worth of New Orleans history – it's slightly overwhelming (the original Jazz Fest poster, transfer documents of the Louisiana Purchase, 1849 broadside advertising '24 Head of Slaves' [individual children for $500 or entire families for $2400], for example) and eminently rewarding.

JACKSON SQUARE
www.jackson-square.com; Decatur & St Peter Sts

Sprinkled with lazing loungers, surrounded by sketch artists, fortune-tellers and traveling showmen and watched over by cathedrals, offices and shops plucked from a Parisian fantasy, Jackson Sq is one of America's great town greens and the heart of the Quarter. The identical, block-long Pontalba Buildings overlook the scene, and the nearly identical Cabildo and Presbytère structures flank the impressive St Louis Cathedral, which fronts the square. In the middle of the park

The Jackson monument, by sculptor Clark Mills, rears in front of St Louis Cathedral at Jackson Sq

There are plenty of ways to soak up New Orleans without drying up your wallet. A few of our favorites:
> Window-shopping on Magazine St (p19)
> Dipping your toes into Bayou St John (p107)
> Feeling like a student again on Tulane's campus (p90)
> Strolling through the city's cemeteries; try St Louis Cemetery (p107)
> Free concerts in Jackson Sq (opposite)

stands the Jackson monument – Clark Mills' bronze equestrian statue of the hero of the Battle of New Orleans, Andrew Jackson, which was unveiled in 1856. The inscription, 'The Union Must and Shall be Preserved,' was added by General Benjamin Butler, Union military governor of New Orleans during the Civil War, who basically wanted to rub it into the occupied city's face (it worked). Free music often happens here, or near here, on a fairly regular basis.

NEW ORLEANS PHARMACY MUSEUM
☎ 565-8027; www.pharmacymuseum.org; 514 Chartres St; adult/concession $5/4; 10am-2pm Tue & Thu, to 5pm Wed, Fri & Sat
This beautifully preserved shop was established in 1816 by Louis J Dufilho at a time when the

pharmaceutical arts were, shall we say, in their infancy. The museum claims Dufilho was the nation's first licensed pharmacist, although his practices would be suspect today (gold-coated pills for the wealthy; opium, alcohol and cannabis for those who needed to feel better for less money).

PRESBYTÈRE
☎ 568-6968; 751 Chartres St; adult/concession/child under 12 $6/5/free; 9am-5pm Tue-Sun
The lovely Presbytère building, designed in 1791 as a rectory for the St Louis Cathedral, serves as New Orleans' Mardi Gras museum. You'll find there's more to the city's most famous celebration than wanton debauchery – or, at least, discover the many levels of meaning behind the debauchery. There's an encyclopedia's worth of material on the krewes, secret societies, costumes and racial histories of the Mardi Gras tapestry, all intensely illuminating and easy to follow.

ST LOUIS CATHEDRAL
☎ 525-9585; Jackson Sq; donations accepted; 9am-5pm Mon-Sat, 1-5pm Sun
One of the best examples of French architecture in the country is the triple-spired cathedral dedicated to Louis IX, the French

king sainted in 1297, a most innocuous bit of Gallic heritage in the heart of an American city. Besides hosting black, white and Creole Catholic congregants, St Louis has also attracted those who, in the best New Orleanian tradition, mix their influences, such as voodoo queen Marie Laveau. The present cathedral was dedicated on Christmas Eve, 1794, and awarded the rank of minor basilica by Pope Paul VI in 1964.

URSULINE CONVENT
☎ 529-2651; 1112 Chartres St; adult $5, concession $2-4, child under 8 free; ⏱ tours hourly 10am-3pm Tue-Fri, 11:15am, 1pm & 2pm Sat & Sun
One of the few surviving examples of French-colonial architecture in New Orleans (though it probably reflects a design more common to French Canada), this lovely convent is worth a tour for its architectural virtues. It also houses a small museum of Catholic bric-a-brac.

SHOP
BOUTIQUE DU VAMPYRE
Gothic Gifts
☎ 561-8267; www.feelthebite.com; 712 Orleans St; ⏱ 10am-7pm
Dark candles and Gothic gargoyles look down on you, promising a curse of blood and terror and the undead on those who only browse but do not buy its vampire and voodoo themed gifts! Mwahaha! Or…not.

CENTURIES
Antique Prints & Maps
☎ 568-9491; 408 Chartres St; ⏱ 10am-6pm
OK, it's a little stodgy, but flip through the inventory (all of it well organized by theme, date or locale) and you'll realize browsing in this shop is like delving into a historical coffee-table book, with no cheesy reproductions. Particularly interesting are the ancient maps, beautifully drawn with outdated demarcations and the occasional glaring cartographic error – why yes, Asia is apparently half the size of Europe.

FAULKNER HOUSE BOOKSTORE *Specialty Books*
☎ 524-2940; www.faulknerhouse books.net; 624 Pirate's Alley; ⏱ 10am-5:30pm
A business and a bona-fide literary attraction, Faulkner House is an essential stop for any lover of books. The shop is an excellent indie bookstore and something of a literary hub: local authors regularly stop by, and its name is due to the fact the granddaddy of Southern lit himself shacked up here during his New Orleans stint.

☐ HOVÉ PARFUMEUR
Perfume

☎ 525-7827; www.hoveparfumeur
.com; 824 Royal St; ⊗ 10am-5pm
Mon-Sat

Grassy vetiver, bittersweet orange
blossom, spicy ginger…New
Orleans' exotic floras have gra-
ciously lent their scents to Hové's
house-made perfumes for over
70 years. A brief sniffing visit will
leave your head swirling with
images of the Vieux Carré's magnificent past. Thus intoxicated,
you can ask staff to custom-mix a
fragrance for you.

☐ LOUISIANA MUSIC FACTORY
Records & CDs

☎ 586-1094; www.louisianamusic
factory.com; 210 Decatur St; ⊗ 10am-
7pm Mon-Sat, noon-6pm Sun

LMC's selection of new and used
CDs delves deep into the musical
culture of New Orleans and Louisiana, with recordings from the
1900s all the way up to this week.
The region's musical well may be
bottomless, but it almost feels
completely tapped here, from jazz
to zydeco to brass bands. Live performances on Saturday afternoons
really rock the joint.

Faulkner House Bookstore: where book lovers unite

🎭 MASKARADE *Masks*
☎ 568-1018; www.themaskstore.com;
630 St Ann St; ⏱ 10am-7pm
This shop deals in high-quality masks by local and international artisans, and the selection includes everything from the classic *commedia dell'arte* masks from Venice to more way-out designs for that wigged-out-end-of–Mardi Gras state of mind.

EAT
🍴 BAYONA
Contemporary Louisianan $$$
☎ 525-4455; 430 Dauphine St;
⏱ 11:30am-2pm Mon-Fri, 6-10pm Mon-Thu, 6-11pm Fri & Sat

Eggs any way you like them at the Clover Grill

Bayona is the best splurge in the Quarter: rich but not overwhelming, classy and unpretentious, innovative without being precocious, and all around just a very fine spot for a meal. Thank chef Susan Spicer and her army of line cooks – they all seem to have a genuine love for what they do and commitment to their craft. The menu changes regularly, but expect fish, fowl and game done up in what we'd describe as a 'surprisingly pleasant' style – the tastes make you raise an eyebrow, then smile like you've discovered comfort food gone classy.

🍴 CAFÉ DU MONDE *Cafe* $
☎ 800-772-2927; www.cafedumonde .com; 800 Decatur St; ⏱ 24hr
Du Monde is overrated, but you'll probably end up here anyways – it's just too iconic. The café au lait is decent while the beignets (light square-shaped doughnuts dusted with powdered sugar) are inconsistent. If you don't want to feel like just another number in some waiter's shift while Bob and Fran loudly mispronounce 'jambalaya' next to you, visit in the middle of the night, when there's a measure of noir-ish cool as the drunks stumble past.

🍴 CLOVER GRILL *Gay Grill* $
☎ 598-1010; www.clovergrill.com; 900 Bourbon St; ⏱ 24hr
You don't actually have to be gay to eat here or work the counter,

but there is a distinct gay vibe, which is slightly surreal given the '50s-diner atmosphere. Hey, nothing adds to Americana like a prima donna–ish argument between an out-of-makeup drag queen and a drunk club kid. The food isn't anything special, but it's dependable burger-breakfast fare – good for a hangover, or those who can see the hangover approaching.

🍴 COOP'S PLACE *Cajun* $
☎ 525-9053; 1109 Decatur St; ⏱ 11am-1am Sun-Thu, to 3am Fri & Sat

Coop's gets credit for maintaining high standards in the midst of the Quarter, where restaurants know they can get away with serving tourists pap. This could almost be a Cajun dive, but it's more rockered-out. While the food may be country, the attitude is tatted-up aggressive friendliness. Make no mistake, it's a grotty, chaotic place that serves stunning food: rabbit jambalaya, chicken with shrimp and *tasso* (highly seasoned and flavored smoked pork, in a cream sauce, natch) – this is rural, rustic and rich food served at an honest price.

🍴 DICKIE BRENNAN'S
Steakhouse $$$
☎ 522-2467; www.dickiebrennanssteak house.com; 716 Iberville St; ⏱ 11:30am-2:30pm Wed-Fri, 5:30-10pm daily

The best steakhouse in the city is also widely considered one of the best in the country, and so there's not a lot left to say about Dickie's: it does steak, and does it incredibly well. The beef comes with beautifully crafted traditional sauces (béarnaise, hollandaise etc) and, if you like, can be topped with local oysters or shrimp. The sides are also gorgeous (key in any good steakhouse), particularly the Pontalba potatoes, done up with garlic, mushrooms and ham.

🍴 FIORELLA'S
Italian & Louisianan $
☎ 523-2155; 1136 Decatur St; ⏱ 11am-midnight Sun-Thu, to 2am Fri & Sat

If you need to eat right in the Quarter for under $20 a head, Fiorella's and nearby Coop's (left) are as good as it gets. Where Coop's is a Cajun country shack hipster-ed up, Fiorella's is a Sicilian cafe, all red-checkered cloth, run through the same punk-rock wringer. The vibe is 'neighborhood spot,' it's just that the 'hood happens to be the grungy north end of Decatur St. Food is quintessential Italian New Orleans: pastas, pizzas, veal cutlets and, arguably, the best fried chicken in town. Some find it too salty, but we say it's just right, especially with hot sauce.

🍴 GW FINS *Seafood* $$$

☎ 581-3467; www.gwfins.com; 808 Bienville St; ⏱ 5-10pm Sun-Thu, to 10:30pm Fri & Sat

The description 'best seafood in town' doesn't get thrown around lightly here, but we've heard it used by a fair few locals in reference to GW Fins. Maybe 'best upscale seafood' is more accurate. Fins focuses, almost entirely, on fish: fresh caught and prepped so the flavor of the sea is always accented and never overwhelmed. For New Orleans this is light, almost delicate dining – it's a refreshing breath of salty air if you're getting jambalaya-ed out.

🍴 PORT OF CALL *Bar & Grill* $$

☎ 523-0120; 838 Esplanade Ave; ⏱ 11am-late

The Port of Call burger is, simply put, one of the best we've had, anywhere. The meat is unadulterated and, well, meaty, and the burger is enormous – a half pound that easily looks the size, and we mean this, of your face. There are a lot of other menu items, but we can't get enough of that burger-y heaven, and neither can the locals, who willingly wait outside in long lines for a seat (no reservations).

The granddaddies of jazz blowin' the house down at Preservation Hall (p51)

🍴 YO MAMA'S *American* $
☎ 522-1125; www.yomamasbarand
grill.com; 727 St Peters St; ⏱ 11am-3am

'Where we eatin' tonight?' 'Yo Mama's.' Chortle chortle chortle. Now
that *that's* out of the way, let us lay
it on the line: peanut butter and
bacon burger. Honestly, it's great:
somehow the stickiness of the
peanut butter complements the
char-grilled meat. It is incumbent
on you, dear traveler, to eat the
native cuisine of a city. In Hanoi,
that's *pho*, in Marrakesh, tagine,
and in New Orleans: peanut butter
bacon burger.

DRINK

🍸 CAROUSEL BAR *Hotel Bar*
☎ 523-3341; 214 Royal St; ⏱ 11am-late

What's the gimmick at this smart-
looking bar inside the historic
Monteleone hotel? It spins. There
are no bobbing seats or toot-toot
orchestra, but there is a canopy
top hat from the 1904 World's
Fair carousel with running lights,
hand-painted figures and gilded
mirrors. It takes 15 minutes for the
bar to complete a revolution. If it's
spinning too fast, ease up on the
sauce, pal. Careful on your way out.

🍸 FRENCH 75 *Restaurant Bar*
☎ 523-5433; 813 Bienville St; ⏱ 5pm-
late

The bar at Arnaud's is all wood
and patrician accents, but staff are

friendly, down to earth and still
able to mix high-quality drinks
that will make you feel a) like the
star of your own Tennessee Williams play about decadent Southern aristocracy and b) drunk.

🍸 MOLLY'S AT THE MARKET
Pub
☎ 525-5169; www.mollysatthemarket
.net; 1107 Decatur St; ⏱ 10am-6am

Molly's is popular with a certain
breed of lush: journalists. This is
the *Times-Picayune* bar and much
more: also popular with cops, fire-
men and Irish Americans; home of
a fat cat that stares stonily at this
booze-sodden kingdom; heart of
Irish activities in the Quarter (ie St
Patty's Day fun); and provider of
shelf space for the urn containing
the ashes of its founder.

🍸 TONIQUE *Lounge*
☎ 324-6045; 820 N Rampart St;
⏱ 5pm-late

New Orleanians might give us flak
for listing Tonique, as this Quarter
gem remains undiscovered by
the masses. We can't imagine
it becoming a Bourbon St bore,
though – it's too dark, intimate
and classy. On any given night,
off-shift service industry folks
gather here like boozy leopards
to a watering hole (and by 'water'
we mean 'gin'). They smoke and
joke with bartenders they know

NEIGHBORHOODS

FRENCH QUARTER

from previous jobs (it's a small fraternity) and drink some of the best-mixed, strongest cocktails in town – the Sazerac comes highly recommended.

PLAY

⭐ DONNA'S BAR & GRILL
Live Music
☎ 596-6914; www.donnasbarandgrill.com; 800 N Rampart St; cover $5-10; ⏲ shows 10pm-late

Walk down St Ann St toward the lighted arches of Louis Armstrong Park and you'll end up at this humble sweatbox, one of the premier brass-band clubs in the city. A nonstop lineup of top jazz and funky second-line outfits plays weekly gigs. Those who aren't on the bill – someone who copped a gig with a touring band, say – frequently drop in to jam, which always ups the ante.

⭐ LE PETIT THÉÂTRE DU VIEUX CARRÉ *Theater*
☎ 522-2081; www.lepetittheatre.com; 616 St Peter St

Going strong since 1916, Le Petit Théâtre is one of the oldest theater groups in the country. In its Jackson Sq home the troupe offers good repertory, with a proclivity for Southern dramas and special children's programming. Shows are sometimes followed by

MISSISSIPPI RIVERBOATS

New Orleans' current fleet of steamboats are theme-park copies of the old glories that plied the Mississippi River in Mark Twain's day. Gone are the hoop-skirted ladies and waxed-mustachioed gents, replaced with pudgy tourists in white shorts, Bourbon St T-shirts and tennis shoes. Still, few visitors to New Orleans can resist the opportunity to get on the Mississippi and have the old paddle wheeler propel them upriver and back down for a spell. It's a relaxing pastime that's good for the entire family.

The **Creole Queen** (☎ 524-0814, 800-445-4109; www.creolequeen.com; jazz dinner cruise adult/child 6-12/child 3-5 $64/30/10, without dinner $40/15/free) runs a two-hour dinner-and-jazz cruise featuring a live Dixieland jazz combo. Cruises board nightly at 7pm and depart at 8pm. Three-hour cruises to Mardi Gras World (p67) board at 1:30pm daily. For all cruises, passengers board at the Canal St Wharf.

Steamboat Natchez (☎ 586-8777, 800-233-2628; www.steamboatnatchez.com; jazz cruise adult/child $40/20, cruise & dinner adult/teen/child $64.50/32.25/$12.25) is the closest thing to an authentic steamboat in New Orleans today. The *Natchez* is steam-powered and has a bona fide calliope on board (an organist performs your favorite pop classics on the 11:30am and 2:30pm cruises). The evening dinner-and-jazz cruise takes off at 7pm nightly. The *Natchez* boards behind the Jackson Brewery.

an informal cabaret performance, with the cast, audience and a resident ghost (so we hear) mingling over drinks.

⭐ ONE EYED JACKS
Live Music & Dive

☎ 569-8361; www.oneeyedjacks.net; 615 Toulouse St; cover $5-15; ☽ noon-late

If you are thinking 'I could really use a night at a bar that feels like a 19th-century bordello managed by Johnny Rotten,' – well…you're in luck. There's a sense very dangerous women in corsets and men with Mohawks and an army of gypsies with bottles of absinthe could come charging out of the walls at any moment. And the acts, which consist of punk, post

punk and the like, are consistently good, especially if you're tired of brass and jazz.

⭐ PRESERVATION HALL
Live Music

☎ 522-2841; www.preservationhall .com; 726 St Peter St; ☽ 8pm-midnight

White-haired grandpas on tubas, trombones and cornets raise the roof every night. It's worth the discomfort of sitting on the floor – but better if you get in line early to snag a good seat. When it's warm enough to leave the window shutters open, those not fortunate enough to get in can join the crowd on the sidewalk to listen to the sets. No booze or snacks are served.

>FAUBOURG MARIGNY & THE BYWATER

Guess which neighborhood in New Orleans has the highest concentration of heritage buildings in the city? That would be Faubourg Marigny. Now guess which neighborhood has the most 'new' New Orleanians…

The Marigny absorbed many of New Orleans' YURPs (young, urban, rebuilding professionals) following Hurricane Katrina. It's not hard to see why. This 'hood feels quintessentially New Orleans in the sense that it's both historic *and* bohemian; stuffed with rows of pretty shotgun shacks, and also traditionally a magnet for the city's gay population and musicians. This gave the Marigny an edgy cred eagerly sought by new arrivals…an edge that's being subdued perhaps, thanks to the impact of gentrification. Now the new line of hip blended with the working class, artists mixing with mechanics and whites neighboring blacks is more properly found in the Bywater, literally just across the railroad tracks.

FAUBOURG MARIGNY & THE BYWATER

◉ SEE
KKProjects 1 B2
Musicians' Village 2 F1
New Orleans Center for
  Creative Arts (NOCCA) 3 C3
Plessy's Plaque 4 C3
St Roch Cemetery &
  Chapel 5 B1

🛍 SHOP
Electric Ladyland .... (see 19)
Faubourg Marigny
  Book Store 6 A3

Green Project 7 C2
New Orleans Art Supply .. 8 E4

🍴 EAT
Adolfo's 9 A3
Bacchanal 10 F4
Elizabeth's 11 E4
Marigny Brasserie ..... (see 19)
The Joint 12 F4

📺 DRINK
Hi Ho Lounge 13 B2
Mimi's in the Marigny .. 14 C3

R Bar 15 A3
Yuki Izakaya 16 A3

⭐ PLAY
d.b.a. 17 A3
Saturn Bar 18 D2
Snug Harbor 19 A3
Vaughan's 20 F4

GETTING HERE
Bus 5 runs down Dauphine and back up Royal St through the Marigny and the Bywater and extends through the French Quarter on N Peters St. Bus 55 runs on Elysian Fields Ave and down Decatur St through the Quarter. Bus 88 runs across the top of the Bywater and Marigny, on St Claude Ave, and continues along Rampart St. The 2 Riverfront streetcar starts from Esplanade Ave (near the Faubourg Marigny) and edges the Quarter and the Warehouse District.

SEE

KKPROJECTS
☎ 218-8701; www.kkprojects.org; 2448 N Villere St; ⏱ 10am-4pm Sat & Sun, also by appointment

At the rough end of St Roch (the neighborhood north of the Marigny, which runs into the Upper Ninth Ward) is KKProjects, one of the more innovative galleries-arts missions in the city. KK has taken, as of this writing, six abandoned homes and, with the input of the local community, turned them into studios-galleries-structures–works of art that feel both a little out of place and refreshingly welcome in this hard-up corner of town. Examples include a house, floored and roofed with sod and turf, that looks like a hobbit hole in the middle of the ghetto, community gardens and greenhouses.

You'll need to drive or cab out here.

MUSICIANS' VILLAGE
www.nolamusiciansvillage.com; bounded by N Roman, Alvar & N Johnson Sts

One of the most prominent post-Katrina reconstruction projects is this 8-acre tract of some 81 houses built primarily for musicians, a vital component of the city's cultural and economic landscape. The brightly painted homes look like skittles scattered across the cityscape. Their brilliant colors, combined with their appealingly modest design, both blend in with and enliven this corner of the Upper Ninth Ward. The village came about via a collaboration between Branford Marsalis, Harry Connick Jr and Habitat for Humanity, and

PLESSY'S PLAQUE
Just a little ways north of the New Orleans Center for Creative Arts (NOCCA; opposite), at the corner of Press and Royal Sts, is a plaque marking the site where Homer Plessy, in a carefully orchestrated act of civil disobedience, boarded a whites-only train car. That action led to the landmark 1896 *Plessy v. Ferguson* trial, which legalized segregation under the 'separate but equal' rationale. The plaque was unveiled in 2009 by Keith Plessy and Phoebe Ferguson, descendants of the opposing parties in the trial, now fast friends.

WORTH A VISIT: THE LOWER NINTH WARD

The Lower Ninth Ward, just east across the Industrial Canal from the Bywater, was one of the neighborhoods hit hardest by Hurricane Katrina, and for many watching coverage of the storm, the name 'Lower Ninth' became synonymous with destruction and disaster. But residents did not think of their home as just a relief case – they always knew they lived somewhere special.

Roland Lewis, a Ninth Ward native and former streetcar worker and union rep, showcases the heritage of his home in his actual home, which has been converted into the awesome **House of Dance and Feathers** (☎ 957-2678; www.houseofdanceandfeathers.com; 1317 Tupleo St). This museum-turned-community-center brims with exhibits on Mardi Gras Indians, social aid and pleasure clubs (the local black community version of civic associations) and the basic gestalt of this unique American neighborhood. To get here you'll need a car and you'll need to call Lewis beforehand, as the museum is open by appointment only. Donate with generosity when you arrive.

Common Ground Relief (☎ 304-9097; www.commongroundrelief.org; 1800 Deslonde St) is a community rebuilding volunteer organization that provides free legal aid and job training, and works on wetland reclamation projects in this area. Just across the headquarters is one of the uber-modern houses built by Brad Pitt's **Make It Right** (www.makeitrightnola.org) foundation. At St Claude Ave and Cafin St you'll see the **Sankofa Marketplace** (www.sankofamarketplace.org; ☼ 10am-3pm every 2nd Sat), a great community farmer's market.

the volunteer efforts of construction workers and local residents. If you visit, bear in mind this is a living neighborhood; folks can get understandably tetchy if you take pictures of them or their property without asking permission.

🅲 NEW ORLEANS CENTER FOR CREATIVE ARTS (NOCCA)
☎ 800-201-4836; www.nocca.com; 2800 Chartres St

Nocca is one of the best arts high schools in America, and admission to this prestigious institution is by audition only. Students specialize in fields ranging from the visual arts to creative writing to dance to cooking, instructed by artists at the top of their craft. This is a school and as such isn't open to visitors 24/7, but check the website for details on upcoming public performances and gallery shows.

🅲 ST ROCH CEMETERY & CHAPEL
☎ 945-5961; cnr St Roch Ave & N Roman St; ☼ 9am-4pm

One of New Orleans' more interesting cemeteries, and arguably the most eccentric chapel, is dominated by a necropolis and 'relic room' that's a great example of the old Catholic practice of offering fake body parts to the healing power of a sacred site. You'll see all sorts of ceramic body parts (ankles, heads, breasts), prosthetics, leg braces, crutches and false teeth hanging from the walls. these are ex-votos, testaments to the healing power of St Roch. The chapel has been appropriated by syncretic voodoo worshippers as well, and if you take a picture inside, floating orbs may appear in your photo, which could be spirits of the dead, or manifestations of saintly healing power, or dust.

SHOP

🏠 ELECTRIC LADYLAND
Tattoos
☎ 947-8286; 610 Frenchmen St;
🕐 noon-midnight Mon-Sat, 1-9pm Sun
New Orleans is an old port filled with bars, drunks and pirates, right? Then a tattoo is just about the coolest souvenir you can get here. Electric Ladyland is clean, brightly lit and does great-quality ink; customized designs can easily be arranged.

🏠 FAUBOURG MARIGNY BOOK STORE *Specialty Books*
☎ 947-3700; 600 Frenchmen St;
🕐 noon-10pm

The South's oldest gay bookstore is a ramshackle, intellectual spot and a good place to pick up local 'zines and catch up on the New Orleans scene, gay or otherwise. Look for the subtle (enormous) rainbow flag.

🏠 GREEN PROJECT
Sustainable Goods
☎ 945-0240; 2831 Marais St; 🕐 9am-5pm
The Green Project sells salvaged building material at extremely cut-rate costs to New Orleanians, providing cheap housing supplies that also preserve the unique architectural facade of the city. It also runs a recycling center, donates paints and art supplies to schools and artists, plants community gardens and runs garden workshops, and does outreach work in the surrounding neighborhoods.

🏠 NEW ORLEANS ART SUPPLY
Art Supplies
☎ 949-1525; www.art-restoration.com; 3620 Royal St; 🕐 10am-5pm Mon-Fri
If you're one who likes to sketch while traveling, here's a good place to go for a fresh supply of pencils and pads. Surprisingly, it's the most central art store in New Orleans, and it's not a bad one. The shop is an annex of the New Orleans Conservation Guild.

'Big Chief' Cheyenne

Keith Price, Chief Cheyenne of the Young Cheyenne Mardi Gras Indians

How long have you been a member of your tribe? I've been doing this since I was four years old. That's how it works here; you start young and this shit gets passed between family. My father did it and his father and it goes all the way back in my family. **How many days of the week do you spend on your Indian costume?** Days of the week? You mean hours of the day! I'm working on a new costume every day when I ain't wearing the current one. This is a constant thing, and it don't never let up: we always adding to a costume and trying to outdo last year's outfit and the guys in the other tribes. When it get near Mardi Gras, I honestly don't even sleep. **Where do you live, and where does that neighborhood fit in with the city's culture?** We in the Upper Ninth. Where I'm at, like anywhere in this city, all the Indian tribes and the social aid and pleasure clubs and the second lines, all that thing we do, well, to be a part of something in New Orleans you got to know people. I don't care if you white, black, whatever; you can't just walk into something. You know someone and you advance based off them connections. That's the New Orleans way.

EAT

🍴 ADOLFO'S *Italian* $$
☎ 948-3800; 611 Frenchmen St; 🕐 6-11pm Mon-Sat

If you take your girl or guy to this intimate Italian cubby and get nowhere afterwards, your date was too hard to please. Adolfo's is pretty much as romantic as New Orleans gets, and it doesn't miss on food either: it's all working-class Italian-Americano fare with some requisite New Orleans zing. Cheap reds by the carafe emerge from the kitchen and raise a diner's spirits – and if they don't, go back to your little black book.

🍴 BACCHANAL
Wine & Cheese $$
☎ 948-9111; http://bacchanalwine.com; 600 Poland Ave; sandwiches $11, cheese per piece from $5; 🕐 11am-9pm

From the outside, Bacchanal looks like a listing Bywater shack of uncommonly large size; inside, there are racks of wine, deli meat and fridges of sexily stinky cheese sold at just above retail price. We recommend an assemble-your-own cheese plate, to be devoured in the backyard of overgrown garden green, scattered with rusted lawn chairs and tatty fold-outs. It's fun and romantic, especially on warm nights. On chef Sundays, cooks from around the city are invited to guest star in the kitchen and let loose with whatever their talented hearts desire.

🍴 ELIZABETH'S *American* $$
☎ 944-9272; www.elizabeths-restaurant.com; 601 Gallier St; 🕐 11am-2:30pm & 6-10pm Tue-Fri, 6-10pm Sat, 8am-2:30pm Sun

Elizabeth's in the Bywater is deceptively dive-y. It looks like – hell, it is – a neighborhood joint.

Stars and flowers embellish a historic house

But the food tastes as good as the best haute cuisine New Orleans can offer. Dinners go from humble beer-barbecued oysters to refined seared duck with port sherry. Whatever you get, be sure to order some praline bacon on the side. That's bacon fried up in brown sugar and, far as we can tell, God's own cooking oil. It's probably an utter sin to consume. But y'know what? Consider us happily banished from the Garden.

🍴 MARIGNY BRASSERIE $$$
American
☎ 945-4472; www.marignybrasserie.com; 640 Frenchmen St; ⏰ 11:30am-9:30pm Mon-Thu, to 10:30pm Fri & Sat, 11am-9pm Sun

Marigny Brasserie is as chic as the Marigny gets. The food is modern American with a bit of a Louisiana kick; think blackened drum with wild rice and orange cardamom chutney, and roasted lamb with garlic grits. The overarching vibe is friendly, even laid back, but the food is as rich and refined as the sort you find in the city's poshest restaurants.

🍴 THE JOINT *Barbecue* $
☎ 949-3232; www.alwayssmokin.com; 801 Poland Ave; ⏰ 11:30am-2:30pm Mon & Tue, to 9pm Wed-Sat

The Joint's smoked pork has the olfactory effect of the Sirens' sweet song, pulling you, the proverbial traveling sailor, off course from your Ithaca into the gnashing rocks of savory meat-induced blissful death. Devour some ribs or pulled pork or brisket, knock it back with sweet tea in the backyard garden and learn to love life (speaking of which, the Joint does a mean peanut butter pie for dessert).

DRINK

🍸 HI HO LOUNGE *Dive*
☎ 945-4446; 2239 St Claude Ave; ⏰ 5pm-late

The Hi Ho is a perfect Bywater bar, the sort of place where you're as likely to compare tattoos with the guy sitting next to you as witness a local second-line after party. Costume parties and punk concerts seem to take place frequently, and the atmosphere is redolent of a barnyard decorated by a farm full of Jimi Hendrix roadies.

🍸 MIMI'S IN THE MARIGNY
Neighborhood Bar
☎ 872-9868; http://mimisinthemarigny.com; 2601 Royal St; ⏰ 5pm-late

The name of this bar could justifiably change to Mimi's *is* the Marigny; we can't imagine the neighborhood without this institution. It's as attractively disheveled as Brad Pitt on a good day, all comfy furniture, pool tables, an upstairs dance hall decorated like a Creole mansion gone punk, and dim brown lighting like a fantasy in sepia. Everyone knows your name, and very likely what your next drink will be.

R BAR *Neighborhood Bar*
☎ 948-7499; http://royalstreetinn.com; 1431 Royal St; ⏱ 3pm-late
We love this illustrious bar named for R (Royal St, that is). There's a barber chair in the middle of the joint where customers sometimes give (and get) lap dances, free crawfish on Friday nights when the bugs are in season, pool

tables constantly cracking and great music. Basic neighborhood bar bliss.

YUKI IZAKAYA *Sake Lounge*
☎ 943-1122; 525 Frenchmen St; ⏱ 5pm-3am
The sake in Yuki is a little pricey, but if you're going to get destroyed, this is the difference between being blown up in an alcohol explosion and getting honorably executed by a samurai. As you sip your rice wine, chill out to a house-lounge DJ and achieve hipster Zen by watching the subtitled Japanese art-house flicks projected onto the walls.

Great live music will set your ears ringing at the Saturn Bar

PLAY

⭐ d.b.a. *Live Music*
☎ 942-3731; 618 Frenchmen St;
🕐 5pm-4am

It's hard to pick any one great aspect of d.b.a. There's the booze menu, which is extensive enough to double as a draft of *Crime and Punishment*. How about the regular and invited music acts? Listening to John Boutté's sweet tenor, which sounds like birds making love on the Mississippi, is one of the best beginnings to a Saturday night in New Orleans. Or there are Wednesdays with Washboard Chaz, a man who demonstrates how a breastplate and two spoons can be the groundwork for Mozart-level musical genius. Great live music, great drinks – seriously d.b.a., you win.

⭐ SATURN BAR *Live Music & Dive*
☎ 949-7532; 3067 St Claude Ave;
🕐 3pm-midnight

In the solar system of New Orleans' bars, Saturn is planet punk and yet much more. Originally, it was simply an eclectic neighborhood bar where a working-class crew of regulars appreciated, in an un-ironic way, the outsider art and leopard-skin furniture. Then the hipsters started moving in. Today the Bywater community, punk scene and hipster enclaves live together in peace and camaraderie, united by neon lighting, flashy gambling machines and great live music.

⭐ SNUG HARBOR *Live Music*
☎ 949-0696; www.snuggjazz.com; 626 Frenchmen St; 🕐 5pm-late

Snug Harbor is the best jazz club in the city, partly because it usually hosts doubleheaders, and partly because the talent is an admirable mix of legends and hot up-and-comers. Plus, the acoustics and sight lines in this spot are superb. Touring jazz acts often make this their first stop in New Orleans, a testament to the loyalty Snug has built with musicians and patrons.

⭐ VAUGHAN'S *Neighborhood Bar*
☎ 947-5562; 800 Lesseps St; cover $7-10; 🕐 11am-3am daily, shows 11pm Thu

On most nights of the week this is a Bywater dive of the best sort, but stop by on a Thursday: that's when Kermit Ruffins, one of the trumpet-playing kings of New Orleans, brings the house, the neighborhood and likely a surrounding 10-mile radius, *down*. The Ruffins show is one of the best regular live acts in the city, if not the country – everyone dances, laughs and loves in a scene so New Orleans it deserves its own Mardi Gras.

NEIGHBORHOODS

FAUBOURG MARIGNY & THE BYWATER

>CBD & THE WAREHOUSE DISTRICT

Let's be honest: central business districts (CBDs) are rarely anyone's favorite part of town. They're inevitably a concrete canyon, all steel and glass and imposing and unfeeling. And New Orleans' CBD does possess these qualities, for sure. But it's also a little more historically and geographically significant than a cluster of big business blocks. Canal St marks the original 'neutral ground' between the European-Creole French Quarter and the American city that sprung up after the Louisiana Purchase. As such, crossing through the CBD means transitioning between the two parts, European and American, that constitute this city. Besides history, this area encompasses plenty of good restaurants, some of the city's best museums and kids' activities, and the Warehouse District, which has become New Orleans' official arts area. Studio spaces are thick on the ground, making this downtown more diverse than you may think.

CBD & THE WAREHOUSE DISTRICT

SEE
Aquarium of the Americas	1	G3
Civil War Museum	2	E5
Contemporary Arts Center	3	E5
Insectarium	4	F3
Louisiana Children's Museum	5	E5
National World War II Museum	6	E5
Ogden Museum of Southern Art	7	E5
Preservation Resource Center	8	F5

SHOP
Arthur Roger Gallery	9	E5
International Vintage Guitars	10	F4
Jean Bragg Gallery of Southern Art	11	E5
Meyer the Hatter	12	E3
New Orleans Glasswork & Printmaking Studios	13	E4

EAT
Cochon	14	F5
Emeril's	15	F5
Herbsaint	16	E4
Luke	17	E3
Mother's	18	F3
Restaurant August	19	F3

DRINK
Circle Bar	20	D5
Le Phare Bar	21	E3
Loa	22	E3
Swizzle Stick Bar	23	F4
Whiskey Blue	24	F3

PLAY
Howlin' Wolf	25	F5
Le Chat Noir	26	E4
Southern Repertory Theater	27	F3

Please see over for map

GETTING HERE
Bus 11 runs from Canal St along the entire length of Magazine St, to Audubon Park. Bus 42 runs on Canal St through Mid-City all the way to City Park. Bus 10 runs on Tchoupitoulas St to Audubon Park. The 2 Riverfront streetcar runs along the river from the Convention Center and along the entire length of the French Quarter, and the St Charles Ave streetcar runs from Canal St along St Charles Ave through the CBD, the Garden District and Uptown. The 45 streetcar runs on Canal St from the river through Mid-City.

SEE

◉ AQUARIUM OF THE AMERICAS

☎ 581-4629; www.auduboninstitute .org; Canal St; adult $18, concession $11-14; ⏱ 9:30am-5pm

The immense Aquarium of the Americas is one of the country's best. The emphasis is loosely regional, with exhibits that delve beneath the surface of the Mississippi River, Gulf of Mexico, Caribbean Sea and Amazon rainforest. Highlights include Spots, a rare white alligator who usually draws a large crowd around the **Mississippi River Gallery** where he suns himself, and the **Caribbean Reef**, a 30ft-long glass tunnel that runs under a 130,000-gallon tank.

◉ CIVIL WAR MUSEUM

☎ 523-4522; www.confederatemuseum .com; 929 Camp St; adult/concession $7/2; ⏱ 10am-4pm Mon-Sat

This smallish space is still more of a collection of 'things' as opposed to a contemporary, interpretation-driven educational museum. The permanent exhibition includes the second-largest compilation of Confederate artifacts in the world, although the museum is to be commended for newer and temporary exhibits: the section on the Creole black regiments that fought for the Confederacy (many free blacks in New Orleans owned slaves) is particularly fascinating.

Fishy business at the Aquarium of the Americas

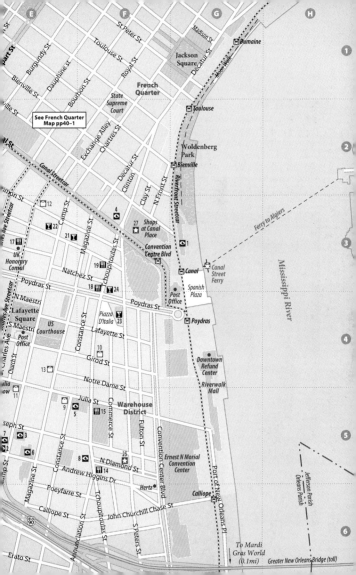

St Peter St
St Peter St
Toulouse St
Burgundy St
Dauphine St
Royal St
Bourbon St

Jackson
Square

**French
Quarter**

State
Supreme
Court

See French Quarter
Map pp40–1

Exchange Alley
Chartres St

Canal St

Clinton
Clay St
N Front St
Decatur St

Canal Streetcar

12

22

21

4

27 Shops
at Canal
Place

Convention
Centre Blvd

1

Camp St

Magazine St

Tchoupitoulas St

17
UK
Honorary
Consul

Natchez St

19

18 24

Poydras St

Piazza
D'Italia
23

Lafayette
Square

US
Courthouse

Constance St

N Maestri

S Maestri

Post
Office

10

Girod St

13

Notre Dame St

11

Julia St

9

5

15

Commerce St

seph St

7

3

2

6

8

N Diamond St

25

14

Andrew Higgins Dr

Hertz

Magazine St

Constance St

Poeyfarre St

Tchoupitoulas St

Calliope St

John Churchill Chase St

S Peters St

BUS
90

Erato St

Annunciation St

Dumaine

Toulouse

Woldenberg
Park

Bienville

Riverfront Streetcar

Canal

Canal
Street
Ferry

Spanish
Plaza

Post
Office

Poydras

Poydras St

Lafayette St

Downtown
Refund
Center

Riverwalk
Mall

**Warehouse
District**

Convention Center Blvd

Fulton St

Ernest N Morial
Convention
Center

Port of New Orleans Pl

Calliope

To Mardi
Gras World
(0.1mi)

Greater New Orleans Bridge (toll)

Ferry to Algiers

Mississippi River

Jefferson Parish
Orleans Parish

E
F
G
H

1
2
3
4
5
6

NEIGHBORHOODS

CBD & THE WAREHOUSE DISTRICT

◎ CONTEMPORARY ARTS CENTER

CAC; ☎ 528-3805; www.cacno.org; 900 Camp St; ☼ 11am-4pm Tue-Sun

The CAC, fronted by a soaring ceiling vault of airy space and conceptual metal-and-wooden accents, exhibits a good crop of rotating exhibitions by contemporary local artists, plus a packed events calendar that includes plays, skits, dance and concerts that draw names like Death Cab for Cutie. Admission costs vary according to exhibitions.

◎ INSECTARIUM

☎ 410-2847; www.auduboninstitute .org; 423 Canal St; adult $14, concession $9-11; ☼ 10am-5pm Tue-Sun

This kid-friendly learning center is a joy for budding etymologists, or anyone with some interest in biology. Exhibits are pretty fun: an 'underground' den where the floor feels like soil and a giant worm burrows through the walls, a typical New Orleanian cupboard overflowing with cockroaches (the accompanying history of the city from a roach point of view is pretty hilarious) and a lovely Japanese garden dotted with whispering butterflies.

◎ LOUISIANA CHILDREN'S MUSEUM

☎ 523-1357; www.lcm.org; 420 Julia St; admission $7.50; ☼ 9:30am-4:30pm Tue-Sat, noon-4:30pm Sun

Probably the kid-friendliest place in New Orleans, this museum is like a high-tech kindergarten, where wee ones can play in interactive bliss till nap time. Lots of corporate sponsorship equals lots of hands-on exhibits, like a stocked supermarket, a TV news studio etc.

Seeing behind the mask, Mardi Gras World

NEIGHBORHOODS

CBD & THE WAREHOUSE DISTRICT

MARDI GRAS WORLD
☎ 361-7821; www.mardigrasworld.com;
1380 Port of New Orleans Pl; adult/child
$18/11; ⏰ 8:30am-5pm
The studio of Blaine Kern – 'Mr
Mardi Gras' – who has been making parade floats since 1947, is
a hell of a lot of fun for adults,
perhaps more so for kids. The best
floats in the city are made here,
and you can see them being built
or on display any time of the year
by popping by Kern's facilities,
located just behind the southern
end of the Convention Center.

NATIONAL WORLD WAR II
MUSEUM
☎ 527-6012; www.nationalww2
museum.org; 945 Magazine St; adult
$14, concession $6-8; ⏰ 9am-5pm
Tue-Sat
This grand facility is both a grand
learning institution and fitting
tribute to those who served in
WWII. It's well designed, physically
and thematically, presenting an
admirably nuanced and thorough
analysis of the biggest war of the
20th century. Of particular note
is the D-Day exhibition, arguably
the most in-depth of its type in
the country. Planned expansions
include a USO-style theater and
pavilions dedicated to every
major campaign America partici-
pated in during the war.

OGDEN MUSEUM OF
SOUTHERN ART
☎ 539-9600; www.ogdenmuseum.org;
925 Camp St; adult/concession $10/6;
⏰ 10am-5pm Mon-Sat
New Orleans entrepreneur Roger
Houston Ogden has assembled
one of the finest collections of
Southern art anywhere – far too
large to keep to himself – which
includes huge galleries ranging
from impressionist landscapes
to outsider art quirkiness to contemporary installation work. Visit
on Thursday nights for Ogden
After Hours, which is when you
can pop an Abita beer with an
arts-obsessed crowd in the midst
of the masterpieces.

PRESERVATION RESOURCE
CENTER
☎ 581-7032; www.prcno.org; 923
Tchoupitoulas St; admission free;
⏰ 9am-5pm Mon-Fri
For anyone with a special interest
in the architecture of New Orleans,
this is a great place to get a sense
of the city's historic neighborhoods. The display is modest,
but you can still grab some of
the dozens of pamphlets, free
walking-tour maps and literature
on virtually every part of town.
Engaging staff provide information on everything from cycling
routes to how to secure low-inter-
est loans to buy and restore your

dream shotgun house. Upstairs, a library contains volumes on local history and architecture.

SHOP

▣ ARTHUR ROGER GALLERY
Gallery

☎ 522-1999; www.arthurrogergallery.com; 432 Julia St; ⏱ 10am-5pm Mon-Sat

One of the area's most prominent galleries, Arthur Roger represents several dozen artists from around the South, including Simon Gunning, whose landscapes are haunting records of Louisiana's disappearing wetlands.

▣ INTERNATIONAL VINTAGE GUITARS *Musical Instruments*

☎ 524-4557; 646 Tchoupitoulas St; ⏱ noon-6pm

A small shop specializing in used guitars and amps. The collection usually features a few showpieces, but its stock generally consists of new Fenders, Epiphones and a few Gibsons.

▣ JEAN BRAGG GALLERY OF SOUTHERN ART *Gallery*

☎ 895-7375; www.jeanbragg.com; 600 Julia St; ⏱ 10am-5pm Mon-Sat

This is a good source for the Arts and Crafts–style Newcomb Pottery, which originated at New Orleans' own Newcomb College.

Bragg also deals in classic landscapes by Louisiana painters, and every month she features the work of a contemporary artist.

▣ MEYER THE HATTER *Hats*

☎ 525-1048; 120 St Charles Ave; ⏱ 10am-5:45pm

New Orleans is a hat town, and hats are a good thing. A brim shades the forehead, covers up the sweaty mess the weather turns your hair into and makes you look bad ass. Meyer has a truly astounding inventory of world-class headwear, and it's serious about its goods: clerks shoo away interlopers who come looking for the wrong type of hat at the wrong time of year.

▣ NEW ORLEANS GLASSWORK & PRINTMAKING STUDIOS *Gallery & Glassworks*

☎ 529-7277; www.neworleansglassworks.com; 727 Magazine St; ⏱ 11am-5pm Mon-Fri

In an immense 25,000ft brick building, New Orleans Glasswork & Printmaking Studios is a combination studio and gallery space primarily for glassblowers and stained-glass artisans. Not only can you admire and purchase works here, you can watch artists blow glass, which is pretty impressive.

Lindsay Glatz
Arts Council of New Orleans

How would you describe the change in New Orleans art since Hurricane Katrina? Institutional level and grassroots organizations alike have sprung up to aid the city's cultural recovery. Artists are learning to take action, and this spirit of entrepreneurship has been captured throughout the city in galleries, festivals, markets and public art pieces that did not exist pre-Katrina. **Why have the arts been an engine for regrowth in the city of New Orleans?** Art and culture mean business in New Orleans. We have managed to build a very organic and authentic arts community (see NOCCA, p55) while utilizing arts and culture as an economic engine for the city. It's a tricky balance. Many who came to our aid after Katrina have discovered and fallen in love with New Orleans, resulting in new opportunities for local artists to thrive. **Why should visitors consider purchasing artwork while in New Orleans?** Art is a solid investment and as New Orleans' prestige as an international art center grows, prices will increase. Many galleries and arts markets are located in a 'cultural products district,' meaning that no tax will be charged for a piece of original or limited-edition art. But beyond the economics, art is about experience. We live in a sensory city. From the architecture, food, music, people and colors of the city, art is all around us. Living New Orleans is art and art is the best way to remember this city.

NEIGHBORHOODS

CBD & THE WAREHOUSE DISTRICT

EAT
🍴 COCHON
Modern Cajun $$$
☎ 588-2123; www.cochonrestaurant
.com; 930 Tchoupitoulas St; 🕙 11am-
10pm Mon-Fri, 5:30-10pm Sat
Donald Link's homage to Cajun
culinary roots is deeply rooted
in pig parts, from pork cheeks
stuffed with goat cheese to pig
cracklin' with cane syrup to local
pig stuffed with cracklin', turnips
and cabbage. There are plenty of
other meats on offer, including
rabbit livers on toast, and fantastic
oysters. The food could be overly
rich, but it ends up just hearty and
smoky enough, without being
totally coma-inducing.

🍴 EMERIL'S
Contemporary Creole $$$
☎ 528-9393; www.emerils.com; 800
Tchoupitoulas St; 🕙 6-10pm Mon-Thu &
Sat, 11:30am-2pm & 6-10pm Fri

The noise level at Emeril Lagasse's
flagship is deafening, but hey,
it's all about the food. Go for the
daily specials, although you can't
go wrong with mainstays like
grilled *filet mignon au poivre* (poor
man's steak; steak encrusted with
peppercorns), and the cheese
board with an accompaniment
from the restaurant's eclectic
wine list.

🍴 HERBSAINT
Contemporary Louisianan $$$
☎ 524-4114; www.herbsaint.com; 701
St Charles Ave; 🕙 11:30am-10pm Mon-
Fri, 5:30pm-10pm Sat
This may cause a riot, but Herb-
saint's duck and andouille gumbo
might be the best restaurant
gumbo in town. The rest of the
food ain't too bad either – much
modern bistro fare with dibs
and dabs of Louisiana influence.
Kurobuta pork belly comes with

SUCK DE' HEAD, CHER
If you leave Louisiana without once tasting crawfish, well…imagine visiting Egypt without
seeing the Pyramids. You just did that, dude.
When crawfish are in season – from early December to mid-July, but best from mid-February –
the most popular way to enjoy them is boiled. Being only a few inches in length, you need to eat a
lot to make a meal; about 4lb to 5lb (2kg to 2½kg) of the little creatures per person is usual.
Huh? How do you eat crawfish? That's easy: pinch de' tail and suck de' head, as the over-
used advice goes. That basically means rip the tail off, squeeze the meat out (it can be tricky,
and may require a little tail-peeling), then suck the juices out of the head. This author takes
it a step further and scoops out the yummy, mustardy brains, which has resulted in no few
funny looks. If the little dude has claws, go ahead and crack those open, too.

local white-bean sauce, while frog-legs hop off the pan (sorry, couldn't resist) with a fine herb dusting. Reservations are a good idea if you're coming for dinner.

🍴 LUKE Bistro $$$
☎ 378-2840; www.lukeneworleans.com; 333 St Charles Ave; ⏱ 7am-11pm
John Besh's letter of love to the working-class bistro has an elegantly simple tiled interior and menu that will make you reconsider the limits of Louisiana-French fusion; the primary muse is the smoky, rich cuisine of Alsace, the French-German border. Vanilla-scented duck with lavender honey, white-bean cassoulet and an admirable nod to German meats like *bockwurst* all give us the pleasurable shudders.

🍴 MOTHER'S Southern Deli $$
☎ 523-9656; www.mothersrestaurant.net; 401 Poydras St; ⏱ 8am-8pm
Despite what you may hear, Mother's isn't the best po'boy around, but it did invent the debris po'boy ('debris' being the bits of roast beef that fall into the gravy and get all soft and lovely) and serves the justifiably famous Ferdi Special, loaded up with ham, roast beef and debris. Breakfast is brilliantly done and served in ponderously enormous portions.

🍴 RESTAURANT AUGUST
Contemporary Creole $$$
☎ 299-9777; www.restaurantaugust.com; 301 Tchoupitoulas St; ⏱ 5-9pm Tue-Thu & Sat, 11am-2pm & 5-9pm Fri
August's converted 19th-century tobacco warehouse gets the nod for most aristocratic dining room in New Orleans. Candles flicker soft, warm shades over a meal that will, quite likely, blow your mind. *Pied du cochon* (stuffed pig trotters) with black truffles, pork belly stuffed with crawfish and blood oranges, and a 10-course, three-hour degustation (tasting) menu that local foodies weep over mean this book's contents are actually more beautiful than its substantially attractive cover.

DRINK
🍸 CIRCLE BAR Live Music & Dive
☎ 588-2616; www.circlebarnola.com; 1032 St Charles Ave; ⏱ 4pm-late, shows 11pm
If Anne Rice's Lestat ever became an alcoholic, we imagine his pad would evolve into something resembling the Circle Bar: a sort of Victorian mansion gone disheveled and punk. Live acts, from folk to rock to indie, often occupy the central space, where a little fireplace and a lot of grime speak to the coziness of one of New Orleans' great dives.

CBD & THE WAREHOUSE DISTRICT

� LE PHARE BAR *Lounge*
☎ 636-1891; http://lepharenola.com; 523 Gravier St; ⏰ 5pm-late Tue-Fri, from 9pm Sat

If you can make yourself heard over the thumping bass, you can wax poetic about this posh, candle-lit, stone-floored Scandinavia-style bar to the beautiful people inside. Don't worry; you're still in New Orleans: brass bands have been known to tromp through and all the chic fashionista-ism on display here hasn't translated into anything resembling snobbery.

� LOA *Lounge*
☎ 553-9550; 221 Camp St; ⏰ 5pm-late

Off the lobby of the fashionable International House Hotel, Loa is a great place to grab a daytime drink or nighttime gander. Everyone looks good bathed in the candle-light or city lights seen through the enormous windows. If you practice voodoo, or just like having your back covered, leave an offering at the voodoo altar on your way out.

� SWIZZLE STICK BAR
Restaurant Bar
☎ 595-3305; 300 Poydras St; ⏰ 7am-11pm

A dash of adult fun massaged with heavy levels of quirkiness, the Swizzle is a good spot for an after-work drink or a pre- or post-convention tipple. Or if you need to

get the night going already, order a 'Trouble Tree,' which comes with a little bit of everything, including the potential for a very fun evening.

� WHISKEY BLUE *Lounge*
☎ 207-5016; 333 Poydras St; ⏰ noon-2am Mon, 5pm-2am Tue-Thu, 4pm-4am Fri & Sat, 5pm-midnight Sun

Whiskey Blue is a sleek, sexy bar where people get dressed up like extras in the *Matrix* and sip what very clearly *isn't* a bottle of Dixie under electric blue lighting. If you're missing Manhattan or Miami Beach, Whiskey Blue's waiting for you.

PLAY

☆ HOWLIN' WOLF *Live Music*
☎ 522-9653; www.howlin-wolf.com; 907 S Peters St; cover $5-15; ⏰ 3pm-late Mon-Fri

One of New Orleans' best venues for live blues, alt-rock, jazz and roots music, the Howlin' Wolf always draws a lively crowd. It started out booking local progressive bands, but has become a regular stop for big-name touring acts like the Smithereens and Hank Williams III.

☆ LE CHAT NOIR *Cabaret*
☎ 581-5812; www.cabaretlechatnoir .com; 715 St Charles Ave; cover free-$20; ⏰ 4pm-2am Tue-Sat, shows 8pm

At this smartly accoutered bar and cabaret the beverage of choice is the martini and the entertainment ranges from Edith Piaf reincarnated to comic stage productions. CBD office workers prevail during 'happy hour' (4pm to 8pm), and a mature audience turns out for the evening shows.

⭐ SOUTHERN REPERTORY THEATER *Theater*
☎ 522-6545; www.southernrep.com; 333 Canal St

Though its home in a shopping mall isn't particularly reassuring, this company has established itself as one of the city's best. Founded in 1986, the company performs original works by Southern playwrights. There's not a bad seat in the 150-seat theater.

>GARDEN & LOWER GARDEN DISTRICTS

Lush, overgrown, green and alive: like Miami and Honolulu, New Orleans is an American city that lives in a love-hate relationship with the fertile conditions of her natural geography. Nowhere else in the city is this sense of constant growth, of trees pushing through sidewalks and vines smothering walls, and leaves raining like a summer storm more evident than the appropriately named Garden District. Also growing amid the trees are the Southern mansions and villas of the American settlers who came here following the Louisiana Purchase.

Nearby, the Lower Garden District is a student-y clump of quieter suburban lanes, good affordable restaurants and some of the city's best shopping. North of 'the LGD' is Central City, once the heart of African American New Orleans, now engaged in sustainable rebuilding; and south is the Irish Channel, composed of pretty shotgun shacks and working-class residential blocks.

GARDEN & LOWER GARDEN DISTRICTS

🅖 SEE
God's Vineyard 1 F4
Goodrich-Stanley House 2 F2
Grace King House 3 E3
Joseph Carroll House 4 D4
Lafayette Cemetery 5 C5
McKenna Museum of
   African American Art ..6 D2
Robert Short's House 7 C4
Rosegate 8 D4

🅢 SHOP
Aidan Gill For Men 9 E4
Anton Haardt Gallery ..10 C5
Funky Monkey 11 C6

Simon of New Orleans ..12 E4
Style Lab for Men 13 B6
Trashy Diva 14 E4

🅔 EAT
Café Reconcile 15 D1
Commander's Palace ..16 C4
Delachaise 17 A5
Joey K's 18 C6
Juan's Flying Burrito ...19 F4
Parasol's 20 D5
Rue de la Course 21 C6
Slice 22 E2
Stein's Deli 23 E4
Sucré 24 C6
Surrey's Juice Bar 25 F2

🅨 DRINK
Balcony Bar 26 C6
Bridge Lounge 27 F2
Bulldog 28 C6
Half Moon 29 F4
Rendezvous ....(see 21)
Saint Bar & Lounge 30 F4

🅟 PLAY
Ashé Cultural Arts
   Center 31 D2
Zeitgeist 32 D1

Please see over for map

GETTING HERE
Bus 11 runs from Canal St along Magazine St to Audubon Park. Bus 10 runs on Tchoupitoulas St to Audubon Park. The St Charles Ave streetcar runs from Canal St along St Charles Ave through the Central Business District (CBD), the Garden District and Uptown.

SEE

IRISH CHANNEL
Btwn First & Toledano Sts
The name Irish Channel is a bit of a misnomer. This historic neighborhood has been the home of many German and black residents living together in a truly multiculti gumbo. This is still a working-class cluster of shotgun houses and you may not want to walk around alone at night, but in general it's pleasant for ambling. Come St Pat-

BEST GARDEN DISTRICT BUILDINGS
Some of the most stunning mansions in the city can be found within the Garden District. You can't enter these houses, but they're still fun to gape at.
Robert Short's House (1448 Fourth St)
Joseph Carroll House (1315 First St)
Rosegate (1239 First St) Anne Rice's house.
Grace King House (1740 Coliseum St)
Goodrich-Stanley House (1729 Coliseum St)

ty's day, the biggest block party around takes over Constance St in front of Parasol's Bar (p82).

LAFAYETTE CEMETERY
Washington Ave at Prytania St; 9am-2:30pm
Shaded by magnificent groves of greenery, this cemetery very much has a sense of Southern subtropical Gothic about it. The layout is divided by two intersecting footpaths that form a cross. Some of the wealthier family tombs were built of marble, with elaborate detail rivaling the finest architecture in the district, but most tombs were constructed simply of inexpensive plastered brick. You'll notice many German and Irish names on the aboveground graves, immigrants devastated by 19th-century yellow-fever epidemics.

MCKENNA MUSEUM OF AFRICAN AMERICAN ART
524-1697; www.themckennamuseum.com 2003 Carondelet St; adult $5, concession $2-3; 11am-4pm Thu-Sat, by appointment Tue & Wed
The permanent exhibition at this beautiful little institution is the amassed collecting efforts of Dr Dwight McKenna. Although the displayed work comes from all over the African diaspora, most of it is created by local New Orleans

400 m
0.2 miles

A
Jackson Ave
Phillip St
Freret St
Lasalle St
S Liberty St
Loyola St
Saratoga St
Danneel St
Dryades St
Baronne St
Carondelet St
Harmony St
Toledano St
St Charles Ave
Louisiana
Foucher St
Delachaise St
Coliseum St
Touro Infirmary
Chestnut St
Camp St
Antonine St
Amelia St
Peniston St
Aline St
Louisiana Ave

B
Phillip St
S Liberty St
Simon Bolivar St
Second St
Third St
Fourth St
Harmony St
Eighth St
Seventh St
Sixth St
Pleasant St
Conney St
Louisiana Ave

C
S Liberty St
Fellicity St
Simon Bolivar St
S Saratoga St
Danneel St
Phillip St
Dryades St
Brainard St
Baronne St
Carondelet St
Philip St
Prytania St
Chestnut St
Washington Ave
Magazine St
Constance St
Laurel St

D
Thalia
Central City
S Saratoga St
Rampart St
Oretha Castle Haley
Carondelet St
Jackson
First St
Second St
Chestnut St
Camp St

1
2
3
4
5
6

Central City

15 33. Oretha Castle Haley 31 Puter

6 Carondel

Jackson

4

20

Lafayette Cemetery No 1
7 16
5
Garden District

17

10 Irish Channel

21 18
11 24
26 28

13

See Uptown & Riverbend Map pp88–9

Honoring the dead, Lafayette Cemetery (p75)

Welcome to the metrosexual headquarters of Orleans Parish. It's all about looking stylish, in a well-heeled, masculine sort of way. High-end shaving gear, smart cufflinks and colorful silk ties are sold in front, and there's a popular barber shop ($35 for a trim, $40 for a shave; reserve a week ahead) out back.

🖼 ANTON HAARDT GALLERY
Gallery
☎ 891-9080; www.antonart.com; 2858 Magazine St; 🕐 noon-5pm Fri & Sat
Among the finest galleries to specialize in contemporary folk art from the Deep South features well-known artists like Howard Finster and Clementine Hunter, but you're more likely to come across Lamar Sorrento's cool portraits of blues musicians or Jimmy Lee Sudduth's striking earth-tone figures.

🖼 FUNKY MONKEY
Vintage Clothing
☎ 899-5587; 3127 Magazine St; 🕐 11am-6pm Mon-Sat, noon-5pm Sun
Vintage attire for club-hoppers is on sale in this funhouse of frippery, as well as wigs, shades and jewelry. Annoyingly, it's turned into one of those vintage shops where the secondhand stuff is as expensive as new clothes, but the duds are admittedly hip-to-trip.

artists. Temporary exhibitions tend to be the real standout; examples include photo-portrait essays on black intellectuals Romare Bearden, Ralph Ellison and Albert Murray.

SHOP
🖼 AIDAN GILL FOR MEN
Men's Coiffure
☎ 587-9090; www.aidangillformen .com; 2026 Magazine St; 🕐 10am-6pm Mon-Fri, 9am-5pm Sat

Zachary Youngerman
Project Manager for Groundwork New Orleans, constructing sustainable landscapes

What are some of the important green initiatives going on in New Orleans? The fight by the Gulf Restoration Network (www.healthygulf.org) and others to save the wetlands of coastal Louisiana. Wetlands are nature's storm barrier, reducing surge from hurricanes a foot in height for every couple of miles of healthy marsh. **Why is this stuff so important in post-Katrina New Orleans?** Abandoning New Orleans or leaving it half-built is untenable. Coastal Louisiana is the nation's largest port, based on tonnage and infrastructure. It contributes more than a quarter of domestic oil production and is the country's second largest commercial fishery. **What are some ways a visitor could be involved?** Cut out meat from your diet. Meat takes a lot of energy to produce. Crawfish, shrimp and catfish are abundant in Louisiana and we know how to prepare them. When choosing a restaurant, make sure it uses our local seafood, fruits and vegetables. **Why do you live where you live and what do you like to do in that area?** I live where the Garden District, Lower Garden District and Central City meet. I like to walk and see the changes: rich to poor, residential to commercial, local to tourist. Plus there's some great cafes around, like Rue de la Course (p83) and my favorite date spot, Delachaise (p81).

NEIGHBORHOODS

GARDEN & LOWER GARDEN DISTRICTS

◻ SIMON OF NEW ORLEANS
Eclectica
☎ 561-0088; 2126 Magazine St;
🕑 10am-5pm Mon-Sat

Local artist Simon Hardeveld has made a name for himself by painting groovy signs that are hung like artwork in restaurants all over New Orleans; you'll probably recognize the distinctive stars, dots and sparkles. Out back, a tabletop box contains hand-painted Zulu coconuts – collectors' items in these parts.

◻ STYLE LAB FOR MEN
Men's Clothing
☎ 304-5072; http://stylelabformen.com;
3641 Magazine St; 🕑 11:30am-6pm Mon-Fri, 10:30am-6pm Sat, noon-5pm Sun

No less an authority than *GQ* has declared this the shop where the well-dressed New Orleanian male gets outfitted, in Ben Sherman, Diesel, Trovata and similar labels.

◻ TRASHY DIVA *Clothing*
☎ 299-8777; www.trashydiva.com;
2048 Magazine St; 🕑 1-6pm Mon-Sat

Funky Monkey (p78): a shoe-in for vintage shopping

Diva's specialty is sassy 1940s- and '50s-style cinched, hourglass dresses and belle epoque undergarments – lots of corsets and lacy, frilly stuff for the look of the Suicide Girl of yesteryear, plus retro tops, skirts and shawls reflecting styles plucked from just about every era.

EAT

🍴 CAFÉ RECONCILE Diner $

☎ 568-1157; www.cafereconcile .com; 1631 Oretha Castle Haley Blvd; 🕙 11am-2:30pm Mon-Fri

Café Reconcile fights the good fight. By recruiting at-risk youth to work as kitchen and floor staff, the restaurant is training a generation of New Orleanians to realize their best potential. The food is humble New Orleans fare: red beans and rice, fried chicken and shrimp Creole, all cooked exceedingly well.

🍴 COMMANDER'S PALACE
Creole $$$

☎ 899-8221; www.commanderspalace .com; 1403 Washington Ave; 🕙 11:30am-2pm & 6:30-10pm Mon-Fri, 11:30am-1pm & 6:30-10pm Sat, 10:30am-1:30pm Sun

As elegant as the Garden District it looms over, Commander's is one of the USA's great restaurants. Owner Ella Brennan prides herself on her ability to promote her chefs to stardom: Paul Prud-

homme and Emeril Lagasse are among the alumni who cut their teeth on nouveau Creole cuisine like fig and foie gras beignets and quail with apples stuffed with local blue crab – decadence all around. No shorts or sandals; jackets are preferred for dinner and reservations are required. Don't miss the lunchtime 25¢ martinis.

🍴 DELACHAISE
Wine & Cheese $$

☎ 895-0858; www.thedelachaise.com; 3442 St Charles Ave; 🕙 5pm-late Mon-Sat, 6pm-late Sun

You gotta love Delachaise's cheese menu – the pictograms that explain 'stinky', 'strong' etc are very cute. Small plates are wonderful in their own indulgent way, especially the ridiculously over-the-top grilled cheese sandwich, which is apparently assembled from truffled bread and foie gras–infused cheese (that's a joke, but the thing really does taste that rich).

🍴 JOEY K'S Diner $

☎ 891-0997; www.joeyksrestaurant .com; 3001 Magazine St; 🕙 11am-3pm & 5-8:30pm Mon-Wed, 11am-3pm & 5-9pm Thu & Fri, 11am-4pm & 5-9pm Sat

Just great Southern diner fare: we'll personally vouch that the cheese fries should be patented,

NEIGHBORHOODS

GARDEN & LOWER GARDEN DISTRICTS

GARDENS OUTSIDE THE DISTRICT

New Orleans has always been a green city, at least in terms of color and hue. The climate and the Caribbean-colonial planning philosophy of the city is the cause of a lush overgrowth that is noticeable even in poorer parts of the city. Indeed, the Lower Ninth Ward, which was wiped out by floodwaters, presently looks more like a wilderness than a ghetto. Nature works fast here, and is always sprouting through walls and foundations.

The challenge many New Orleanian plant-lovers face is channeling this awesome fecundity into plots that are attractive and utilitarian. Enter **Parkway Partners** (Map pp64–5, D5; ☎ 620-2224; www.parkwayparntersnola.org; 1137 Baronne St), one of the better NGOs operating in New Orleans at the moment. Besides funding urban tree-planting projects and similar programs, Parkway is looking to expand, with local contribution, its series of community gardens.

At the time of research there were almost 30 such gardens scattered across the city, each one a lovely example of community partnerships and grassroots beautification efforts. All are undoubtedly pretty, but some gardens also serve a functional role: as a source of fresh veg and produce for local tables, and in helping to leech lead out of the local soil (New Orleans has unusually high levels of lead contamination in its soil). There's a full list of active community gardens at www.parkwaypartnersnola.org/gardenlist.html. Some of our other favorites include **Le Jardin du Soleil** (Map pp88–9, H5; 3458 Annunciation St), **Bywater Herb Farm** (Map p53, F3; 4327 N Rampart St) and **God's Vineyard** (928 Felicity St).

while specialties like fried pork chops and white beans and turkey with stuffing, yams and green beans is as satisfying a meal as you'll find for under $20 in the Lower Garden.

🍴 JUAN'S FLYING BURRITO
Mexican $
☎ 569-0000; www.juansflyingburrito.com; 2018 Magazine St; 🕑 11am-10pm Mon-Thu, 11am-11pm Fri & Sat, noon-10pm Sun

The answer to that perennial question, 'What happens when you cross a bunch of skinny-jean-clad hipsters with a tortilla is, ta da: Juan's. The food is about as

authentically Mexican as Ontario, but it's still good. The hefty burritos pack a satisfying punch against your hunger and the margaritas are damn tasty.

🍴 PARASOL'S *Po'boys* $
☎ 899-2054; 2533 Constance St;
🕑 11am-10pm

Parasol's isn't just on the Irish Channel, it sort of is the Irish Channel, serving as community center, nexus of gossip and, natch, watering hole (because, yes, this is first and foremost a bar). But it also serves some of the best po'boys in town, devoured amid a mad, friendly cast of characters both behind and ordering from the bar.

🍴 RUE DE LA COURSE *Cafe* $
☎ 899-0242; 3121 Magazine St;
🕐 7:30am-11pm

This spacious coffee shop is constantly filled with folks on computers banging away on that next term paper, screenplay, email, Facebook post and, er, guidebooks. It's friendly, the coffee is good and, crucially, there are lots of power outlets for your laptop. Cash only.

🍴 SLICE *Pizza* $
☎ 525-7437; www.slicepizzeria.com;
1513 St Charles Ave; 🕐 11am-11pm
Mon-Sat, noon-10pm Sun

Our favorite pizza in New Orleans is thin crust and can be as artisanal or run-of-the-mill as you like: you can opt for something as out there as goat cheese, pesto and anchovies or good ol' pepperoni. Order by the slice (imagine that!) starting at just $2.15.

🍴 STEIN'S DELI *Deli* $
☎ 527-0771; www.steinsdeli.net; 2207
Magazine St; 🕐 7am-7pm Tue-Fri, 9am-
5pm Sat & Sun

Stein's is more of a center for the city's Jewish population than any one synagogue. If lunch, for you, rests on quality sandwiches, cheese and cold cuts, this is as

good as New Orleans gets. Owner Dan Stein is a fanatic about keeping his deli stocked with great Italian and Jewish meats and cheeses and some very fine boutique beers: the man even hosts his own beer-brewing classes. We tip our hats to you, sir.

🍴 SUCRÉ *Chocolate* $$
☎ 520-8311; www.shopsucre.com; 3025
Magazine St; 🕐 7:30am-11pm

Sucre sells the sort of chocolate you'd think was hidden behind secret government titanium vaults – dollops of single espresso beans encased in bittersweet darkness like a silk kiss and all that other food porn adjective-heavy verbiage. Some of Sucré's 21-piece boxes run to as much as $68.

🍴 SURREY'S JUICE BAR
American $
☎ 524-3828; www.surreyscafeandjuice
bar.com; 1418 Magazine St; 🕐 8am-
3pm

Here comes the controversial assessment: Surrey's does the best cheap breakfast, and perhaps the best breakfast period, in New Orleans. *Boudin* (Cajun sausage) biscuits, eggs scrambled with salmon and a shrimp-grits-and-bacon dish that should be illegal – you won't go wrong. And the juice, as you might guess, is blessedly fresh.

DRINK

BALCONY BAR *Bar*

☎ 894-8888; 3201 Magazine St; noon-late Mon, 4pm-late Tue-Sat, 4pm-midnight Sun

This student-centric pub is a good place for pizza, carousing and sitting on the titular balcony while watching the Magazine St parade march by on balmy nights.

BRIDGE LOUNGE *Neighborhood Bar*

☎ 299-1888; http://bridgeloungenola.com; 1201 Magazine St; 4pm-late Mon-Fri, 6pm-late Sat & Sun

We respect any bar that has dedicated dog nights – Tuesday in the case of Bridge Lounge, which is also a center for the local singles scene due in no small part to friendly bar staff who mix a mean cocktail. Try the mint julep, one of the better made in town.

BULLDOG *Neighborhood Bar*

☎ 891-1516; www.draftfreak.com; 3236 Magazine St; 2pm-late Mon-Thu, 11:30am-late Fri & Sat

The Bulldog keeps a very respectable menu of microbrews served draught, which demands some respect. The best place to sink a pint or a pitcher is in the courtyard, which gets fairly packed with the young and the beautiful almost every evening when the weather is warm enough.

HALF MOON *Dive*

☎ 522-7313; 1125 St Mary St; 11am-4am

On an interesting corner, just half a block from Magazine St, the Half Moon beckons with a cool neighborhood vibe. The place is good for a beer, short order meal or an evening shooting stick.

RENDEZVOUS *Neighborhood Bar*

☎ 891-1777; 3101 Magazine St; 2pm-late Sun-Thu, 4pm-late Fri & Sat

Very much a locals' hangout, the Rendezvous is sort of made for just that – hopefully with a good group of friends. The pool tables and Golden Tee arcade game keep the collegiate crowd happy, while yuppie types stumble toward their favorite bartenders for good beer and banter.

SAINT BAR & LOUNGE *Dive*

☎ 523-0500; www.thesaintneworleans.com; 961 St Mary St; 6pm-late

Ah…great backyard beer garden enclosed in duck blinds, tattooed young professionals, Tulane students, good shots, good beers, good times and a photo booth that you will inevitably end up doing something silly in before the night is through. It's not the cleanest bar (nickname: the Taint), but it sure is a fun one.

PLAY

⭐ ASHÉ CULTURAL ARTS CENTER

Multidisciplinary Arts Center

☎ 569-9070; www.ashecac.org; 1712 Oretha Castle-Haley Blvd

An important anchor for the local African American community, Ashé (from a Yoruban word that could loosely be translated as 'Amen') regularly showcases performances, art exhibitions, photographs and lectures with an African/African America/Caribbean focus.

⭐ ZEITGEIST

Multidisciplinary Arts Center

☎ 352-1150; www.zeitgeistinc.net; 1618 Oretha Castle-Haley Blvd

Independent film screenings, arts and activism workshops, a rotating exhibition space that hosts everything from post-Katrina photography to Free Palestine lectures – you get the idea. Almost every night at this 'multidisciplinary arts center' is packed with something educational, controversial, creative or all of the above.

>UPTOWN & RIVERBEND

If you're not local, chances are you haven't heard of this part of the city, so we feel a little guilty for potentially blowing the top off one of the best-kept secrets in town. Namely: Uptown is possibly the most pleasant neighborhood in New Orleans. Let's parse that word 'pleasant.' It doesn't necessarily mean most fun or safest or prettiest – more like the awesome intersection of the near-attainment of these qualities, to the point that Uptown is just supremely livable. It helps that there's great shopping and restaurants everywhere you turn, and beautiful stretches of mansions and cottages throughout.

North of here, Riverbend and its surrounds snake around Tulane and Loyala universities. Unsurprisingly, this is one of the most student-oriented parts of New Orleans, mixing up cheap eats, good bars and an *Animal House* meets Southern-aristocracy atmosphere that can be pretty intoxicating, in both the figurative and literal sense of the word.

UPTOWN & RIVERBEND

🅒 SEE
Audubon Zoological
  Gardens 1 B5
Touro Synagogue 2 F4
Tulane University 3 C3

🅐 SHOP
C Collection 4 B2
Dirty Coast 5 D5
Maple Street Bookshop ..6 C2
Pied Nu 7 D5
Retroactive 8 D5
Shoefty 9 C5
Sweet Pea and Tulip 10 D5
Yvonne La Fleur 11 B2

🅔 EAT
Boucherie 12 C1
Brigtsen's Restaurant ..13 B1
Camellia Grill 14 B2
Casamento's 15 F5
Cooter Brown's Tavern
  & Oyster Bar 16 B2
Dante's Kitchen 17 B1
Domilise's Po-Boys 18 E6
Frankie & Johnny's 19 D6
Gautreau's 20 E4
Guy's 21 E5
Hansen's Sno-Bliz 22 E6
Ignatius 23 F5
Jacques-Imo's Café 24 B1
La Crepe Nanou 25 C5
Mat & Naddie's 26 B1
Patois 27 C5
St James Cheese Co 28 E5

Taqueria Corona 29 D5
Tee-Eva's Creole Soul
  Food 30 F5

🅨 DRINK
Boot 31 C2
Columns Hotel 32 G4
Cure 33 E3
F&M Patio Bar 34 E6
Le Bon Temps Roulé 35 E5
Ms Mae's ....(see 15)
Snake & Jake's 36 C2
St Joe's Bar 37 D5

⭐ PLAY
Maple Leaf Bar 38 B1
Tipitina's 39 F6

Please see over for map

SEE
☉ AUDUBON PARK & ZOOLOGICAL GARDENS
☎ 581-4629; www.auduboninstitute
.org; adult $12, concession $7-9; 6500
Magazine St; ☺ 9am-5pm

Long acknowledged as one of
the country's best zoos, this
garden-like park is the heart of
the Audubon Institute, which also
maintains the Aquarium of the
Americas (p63) and the Insectarium (p66). While international
in focus, the exhibits on native
flora and fauna sing the most,

GETTING HERE
Bus 11 runs from Canal St along Magazine St to Audubon Park. Bus 10 runs on
Tchoupitoulas St to Audubon Park. Bus
12 runs along St Charles Ave, and the St
Charles Ave streetcar runs from Canal St
along St Charles Ave through the Central
Business District (CBD), the Garden District and Uptown.

particularly the **Louisiana Swamp**
bayou re-creation. **Reptile Encounter**
humanizes (as it were) our scaly
friends, and there are all sorts of
rides, such as the **Swamp Train** ($5)

Keep it clean, boys: the Hygeia fountain at the Audubon Zoological Gardens

NEIGHBORHOODS

UPTOWN & RIVERBEND

THE ST CHARLES AVENUE STREETCAR

New Orleanians can lay claim to the oldest continuously operating street railway system in the world – it sure feels like it at times when you're waiting for the next pickup from the **St Charles Ave Streetcar**. OK, to be fair, while the service can be inconsistent, in general it's pretty good and a ride in the old-time carriages is atmospheric as hell. The streetcar began life as the nation's second horse-drawn streetcar line, the New Orleans & Carrollton Railroad, in 1835. The line was among the first systems to be electrified when the city adopted electric traction in 1893. Now it's one of the few streetcar lines in the US to have survived the automobile era. The fleet of antique cars survived the hurricanes of 2005 and today full service has been restored all the way to South Carrollton Avenue. Fare is a flat $1.25, and the service runs from 6am to 11pm, with cars every 15 minutes or so (supposedly).

and the **Safari Simulator** ($5) for kids, or kids at heart.

⊙ LEVEE PARK
The earthen levee that follows the curve of the Mississippi River from Audubon Park to Jefferson Parish is a public right-of-way. It's a nice spot for walking, jogging or biking, but views onto the river are occasionally only so-so and there aren't enough paths connecting the levee to the street below (if you try to cross off-path, you may find yourself ankle deep in Mississippi mud). Still, it's a good little green space.

⊙ TOURO SYNAGOGUE
☎ 895-4843; www.tourosynagogue .com; 4238 St Charles Ave
Founded in 1828, Touro is the oldest synagogue in the city and the oldest in the USA outside of the original 13 colonies. It bears a

slight resemblance to a red brick Byzantine temple, with its squat buttresses and bubbly domes. The local congregation began as an amalgamation of local Spanish-descended Jews and German Jewish immigrants, a relatively rare mixed lineage in American Judaism.

⊙ TULANE UNIVERSITY
☎ 865-4000; www.tulane.edu; 6823 St Charles Ave
One of the south's premier universities boasts 22,000 students in 11 colleges and schools and big-name alumni like former French president Jacques Chirac, Republican firebrand Newt Gingrich, Jerry Springer and a very long list of Louisiana governors, judges and assorted politicos. The school sprawls across an attractive cluster of greens, red-brick buildings and quads north of Audubon Park – this

is one of the prettiest colleges in the country, and well worth a stroll for anyone wanting to reclaim a sense of school days (or daze).

SHOP

⬛ C COLLECTION *Boutique*

☎ 861-5002; 8141 Maple St; ⏱ 10am-6pm Mon-Sat

The female population of Tulane University (and women of the Riverbend region in general) are kept fashionable and smiling thanks to the cute dresses, chunky belts, skinny pants and hip-hugging shorts on offer in this converted house-cum-boutique.

⬛ DIRTY COAST
New Orleans Clothing

☎ 324-3745; http://dirtycoast.com; 5704 Magazine St; ⏱ 10am-7pm

You're not a cool new New Orlean-ian if you haven't picked up one of the clever T-shirts or bumper stickers ('Make Wetlands, Not War') – all related to local issues, inside jokes and neighborhood happenings – in this ridiculously cool store.

⬛ MAPLE STREET BOOKSHOP
Books

☎ 866-4916; www.maplestreetbook shop.com; 7523 Maple St; ⏱ 9am-7pm Mon-Sun, 11am-5pm Sun

Shopkeeper Rhonda Kellog Faust advocates for antiracism group

Erace and is a storehouse of local knowledge. The business, which includes a children's bookstore, was founded by her mother and aunt over 30 years ago and is one of the most politically progres-sive, well-stocked bookstores in the city.

⬛ PIED NU *Boutique*

☎ 899-4118; www.piednuneworleans .com; 5521 Magazine St; ⏱ 10am-5pm Mon-Sat

If you need a hand-poured candle that lasts 60 hours, try one of the sweet-smelling Diptyques on sale here. As you soak up that vanilla-scented goodness, browse through elephant-printed cotton T-shirt dresses, cinched poet dresses and low-joe sneakers. Set it off with tiny leaf earrings and you're almost as endearing as this precious boutique.

⬛ RETROACTIVE
Vintage Jewelry

☎ 895-5054; 5414 Magazine St; ⏱ 10am-6pm

Once you've ducked in through the vintage handbags and crazy hats that literally hang from the ceiling, slow down a bit to inspect the jaw-dropping selection of cos-tume jewelry. Beautiful glass and Bakelite pieces plucked from the mid-20th century cost anywhere from $20 to $500.

☐ SHOEFTY Shoes & Accessories
☎ 896-9737; 6010 Magazine St;
🕐 10am-6pm Mon-Sat

Shoe stores tend to be aimed at women, and there's no doubt girls will be in footwear heaven here amid the strappy, the pump-y, the chunky and the tottering heel-y. But metrosexual men (or dragged-along boyfriends) will also find cool kicks that may convince some of us that it's acceptable to own more than one pair of sneakers.

☐ SWEET PEA AND TULIP
Boutique
☎ 899-4044; 802 Nashville Ave;
🕐 10am-6pm Mon-Sat, 11am-5pm Sun

Sweet Pea and Tulip – jeez, the name alone – is almost painfully cute. You will be, too, if you deck yourself out in the frock-y, fun contemporary and retro-inspired outfits that stack these shelves.

☐ YVONNE LA FLEUR
Classic Clothing
☎ 866-9666; www.yvonnelafleur.com; 8131 Hampson St; 🕐 10am-6pm Mon-Sat, to 8pm Thu

They just don't make them like this anymore – neither the clothes, millinery or lingerie for sale in Yvonne La Fleur nor Yvonne herself, the definition of steel in silk. She's an amazing businesswoman who has outfitted generations of

I WENT TO NOLA & ALL I GOT WAS…
Centuries (p44) A 19th-century lithograph.
Electric Ladyland (p56) A tattoo.
Faulkner House Bookstore (p44) *The Sound and the Fury.*
Louisiana Music Factory (p45) Local music.
Maskarade (p46) Carnival masks.
Meyer the Hatter (p68) A fedora.
Simon of New Orleans (p80) A hand-painted sign and some Zulu coconuts.
Trashy Diva (p80) A bustier.

local ladies for their weddings, debuts and race days. She makes her own perfumes and gorgeous hats, overflowing with silk flowers, that seem to belong to another era. Wear some of Yvonne La Fleur's classic couture as you explore the city that inspires Yvonne's unique look.

EAT
☐ BOUCHERIE
Modern American $$
☎ 862-5514; www.boucherie-nola.com; 8115 Jeannette St; 🕐 11am-3pm & 5:30-9pm Tue-Sat

Can you improve upon a Krispy Kreme donut? We didn't think so, but along comes Boucherie's signature dessert: Krispy Kreme bread pudding. Damn. There's more wacky deliciousness on this unique menu: darkly sweet and savory barbecued shrimp and grits cakes; stinky, gooey, glorious garlic parmesan fries; and a magical duck confit with truffled baby salad.

BRIGTSEN'S RESTAURANT
Contemporary Cajun $$$
☎ 861-7610; www.brigtsens.com; 723 Dante St; ☽ 5:30-10pm Tue-Sat

Frank Brigtsen terms his cooking 'modern Louisiana cuisine,' and those in search of haute-Cajun will not be disappointed. Look for the roast duck with cornbread dressing and honey-pecan gravy, or beef tournedos in a *tasso* (highly seasoned and flavored smoked pork) wine sauce, served up with a craftsman's expertise and an artist's eye in a lovely double shotgun shack by the river.

CAMELLIA GRILL
Grill & Diner $
☎ 309-2679; www.camelliagrill.net; 626 S Carrollton Ave; ☽ 9am-1am Mon-Thu, 9am-3am Fri, 8am-3am Sat, 8am-1am Sun

The other great thing about this spot, besides its excellent diner burger-chili-Reuben fare, is it's the sort of place where the black staff look like 50 Cent, the white staff look like the Ramones and they all call each other – and you – 'baby.' All the time. Plus, they dress in tux shirts and black bow ties, as if this place couldn't be any wonderfully weirder.

CASAMENTO'S *Seafood* $
☎ 895-9761; http://casamentosrestaurant.com; 4330 Magazine St; ☽ 11am-2pm & 5:30-9pm Tue-Sat, closed in summer

This is as good as oysters get in New Orleans: a 1949 soda shopesque sparkling white interior and a big man behind a marble counter shucking shells to order. Get your raw boys with a beer, or try the famous oyster loaf (a sandwich of breaded and fried oysters on white bread). Cash only.

Little 'uns tucking in at the Camellia Grill

🍴 COOTER BROWN'S TAVERN & OYSTER BAR *Oysters & Grill* $

☎ 866-9104; www.cooterbrowns.com; 509 S Carrollton Ave; 🕒 11am-1am

Cooter's is open late, does mean cheese fries, whips out a killer chili cheese dog and has one of the best beer selections in the city. But our long, lingering romance with Mr C Brown is attributable to his oyster bar. The boys are shucked to order here, plump and cold and, at $8 for a dozen, an absolute steal.

🍴 DANTE'S KITCHEN
Contemporary Louisianan $$$

☎ 861-3121; www.danteskitchen.com; 736 Dante St; 🕒 5:30-10pm Wed-Mon, 10:30am-2pm Sat & Sun

Dante's specializes in melding French, American and Louisiana traditions: pork shoulder with red *boudin* (Cajun sausage) dirty rice and maple-glazed chicken with potato-bacon hash cake are good examples, but it's the Sunday brunch we enjoy most. Debris and poached eggs on a caramelized onion biscuit, topped with a demi-glacé hollandaise sauce is a pretty unbelievable way to start your day, unless you opt for the bread pudding French toast.

🍴 DOMILISE'S PO-BOYS
Po'boys $

☎ 899-9126; 5240 Annunciation St; 🕒 11am-7pm Mon-Sat

Domilise's is everything that makes New Orleans great: a dilapidated white shack by the river serving Dixie beer, staffed by folks who've worked here for decades, prepping if not the best po'boys in the city, at least the best seafood sandwich. Belly up to the bar, get us another Dixie and welcome home. Cash only.

🍴 FRANKY & JOHNNY'S
Cajun $

☎ 899-9146; 321 Arabella St; 🕒 11am-9pm

If you took a New Jersey Italian diner, plopped it by the Mississippi River and replaced the pizza with red beans and rice and fine crawfish off the bayou, there, friends would be Franky & Johnny's. It's a local favorite for casual Cajun food. Opt for the daily specials.

🍴 GAUTREAU'S
Modern American $$$

☎ 899-7397; 1728 Soniat St; 🕒 6-10pm Mon-Sat

Chef Sue Zemanick has seemingly won every award a rising star can garner in American culinary circles ('Top 10 Best New Chef' in *Food & Wine* magazine and 'Chef of the Year' in *New Orleans* magazine, among others). Gautreau's, her HQ, is unsigned and tucked away in a residential neighborhood. Inside, savvy diners dine on fresh, modern American fare – gnocchi with truffled parmesan cheese and grouper in a salsa verde, for example – content they're enjoying a treasure of the local culinary landscape as yet undiscovered by tourists.

🍴 GUY'S Po'boys
☎ 891-5025; 5259 Magazine St; ⏱ 11am-4pm Mon-Sat

Guy's owner is also the cashier, head shopper, chef and prep staff. Ergo your sandwich is made fresh and to order, with a level of attention you don't get anywhere else in the city. Even when the line is out the door – and it often is – each po'boy is painstakingly

crafted. So yes, that loaf will take a while. But damn is it worth it.

🍴 HANSEN'S SNO-BLIZ
Snowballs

☎ 891-9788; http://snobliz.com; 4801 Tchoupitoulas St; ⏱ 1-7pm Tue-Sun

The snowball (shaved ice with flavored syrup) is New Orleans' favorite dessert, and Hansen's, in business since 1939, may be New Orleans' favorite ball. Founder Ernest Hansen, who passed away after Hurricane Katrina, patented the shaved ice machine, and his granddaughter, Ashley, runs the family business, doling out shaved ice covered with syrups in flavors from root beer to cream of nectar.

Cooter Brown's Tavern & Oyster Bar... Where oysters open up to you

IGNATIUS *Creole* $

☎ 896-2225; 4200 Magazine St;
🕑 9am-9pm

One of New Orleans' better small neighborhood joints, Ignatius does standbys like alligator po'boys and red beans and rice very well, if not exceptionally. Brunch is the main draw, especially omelets groaning under crab meat and crawfish étouffée.

JACQUES-IMO'S CAFÉ
Louisianan $$$

☎ 861-0886; www.jacquesimoscafe
.com; 8324 Oak St; 🕑 5:30-10pm Mon-Sat

If cornbread muffins swimming in butter aren't rich enough, how about steak smothered in *bleu* cheese and bacon? Or the insane yet wickedly brilliant alligator sausage cheesecake? That's the whole attitude at Jack Leonardi's exceedingly popular restaurant: die, happily, with butter and heavy sauces sweating out of your pores. Jack can often be seen in the kitchen (which you walk through to get to the dining room) cooking in his boxer shorts – always a sign of quality.

LA CREPE NANOU *French* $$

☎ 899-2670; www.lacrepenanou.com;
1410 Robert St; 🕑 6-10:30pm Mon-Thu,
to 11pm Fri & Sat

New Orleans is a city that loves its bistros, but it all too often Creole-

izes steak *frites*, and sometimes, you want your sweetbreads simple and unadorned by crawfish. Crepe Nanou feels your pain; it stays true to classically French form here, slinging mussels, steaks, excellent *frites* and, of course, some very fine crepes.

MAT & NADDIE'S
Modern Southern $$$

☎ 861-9600; www.matandnaddies
.com; 937 Leonidas St; 🕑 11am-2pm &
5:30-9:30pm Mon, Thu & Fri, 11am-2pm
Tue & Wed, 5:30-9:30pm Sat

Everything comes together here. A beautiful riverfront cottage with a Christmas-light bedecked patio in the back, rich, innovative, even amusing, food like duck-fat-fried chicken with waffles and pecan sweet-potato pie (all crazy delicious) and just damn friendly staff and service. M&N's is kind of weird – high-quality topped with quirkiness– and honestly one of our favorite splurges in the city.

PATOIS *French-Creole* $$$

☎ 895-9441; http://patoisnola.com;
6078 Laurel St; 🕑 5:30-10pm Wed, Thu
& Sat, 11:30am-2pm & 5:30-10pm Fri,
10:30am-2pm Sun

One of the hottest names on local foodies' lips, Patois serves French haute with a New Orleans accent (hence 'patois'). Roasted pheasant in foie gras emulsions and new twists on surf-and-turf, like pork belly with scallops, pop up on an ever-shifting, always excellent menu. Customers – largely locals – are here for good food in an old house. You feel like you're at a friend's dinner party rather than a restaurant.

ST JAMES CHEESE CO
Deli & Cheese $

☎ 899-4737; www.stjamescheese.com; 5004 Prytania St; ⏱ 11am-6pm Mon-Thu, to 8pm Fri & Sat, to 4pm Sun

St James was founded by an Englishman obsessed with all the right things: namely, meat and fermented milk product. There's a veritable atlas worth of cheese on sale, plus excellent sandwiches like mozzarella with basil pesto and salami. Hosts frequent cheese tastings.

TAQUERIA CORONA
Mexican $

☎ 897-3974; 5932 Magazine St; ⏱ 11:30am-2pm & 5-9:30pm

Corona serves the best Mexican food in town. It's a friendly spot that gets jam packed every evening with families, young Uptown professionals and Tulane kids chowing down on some excellent burritos (we like the bean), tacos (go for the fish or chorizo) and flautas (mmm, the shrimp).

TEE-EVA'S CREOLE SOUL FOOD *Creole* $

☎ 899-8350; 4430 Magazine St; ⏱ 11am-6pm Mon-Sat, noon-5pm Sun

Just search out the little yellow shack with the singing lady painted on the side. That's Tee-Eva, who once sang backup to late, great local legend Ernie K-Doe. Now she whips up snowballs, pralines and some fine hot lunches like baked chicken, plates of red beans and rice, and sweet and savory pies.

DRINK
BOOT *Bar*

☎ 866-9008; 1039 Broadway St; ⏱ 11am-late

The Boot, practically located within Tulane's campus, could double as student housing for that university. If you're within the vicinity of age 21, this place is a lot of fun; otherwise, you might think you'd accidentally stumbled into Athens what with all the Greeks (ie frat boys and sorority girls).

COLUMNS HOTEL *Hotel Bar*

☎ 899-9308; www.thecolumns.com; 3811 St Charles Ave; ⏱ 3pm-midnight Sun-Thu, to 2am Fri & Sat

The Columns looks like a set piece from *Gone With the Wind*, as do a lot of its patrons. But it's not that aristocratic – more like a place where college students and just-graduates act the part of the Southern upper crust. One of those places where you could wear a full seersucker ensemble and not feel self-conscious.

▼ CURE Bar
☎ 302-2357; http://curenola.com; 4905 Freret St; ⏷ 5pm-midnight Sun-Thu, to 2am Fri & Sat

It's rare that a genuinely innovative bar comes along, so hooray for Cure. Set in a smooth and polished space with a Zen outdoor garden, this is where you come for a well-mixed drink, period. Try the appropriately dubbed Howitzer (bourbon, bitters, lemon juice and magic), which will pretty much blow your sobriety to smithereens. The staff take mixology and atmosphere seriously here, and in the evening you need to come correct: no shorts and sandals for guys, guys.

▼ F&M PATIO BAR College Bar
☎ 895-6784; www.fandmpatiobar.com; 4841 Tchoupitoulas St; ⏷ 24hr

On weekends, every college student in Louisiana tests the structural integrity of F&M's leopard-print pool tables by dancing on them. For the rest of the week this is a really nice place, with good pool going (on the aforementioned tables), a nice grill slinging killer cheese fries and a semi-out-door area that's well-suited for a cold beer under the hot sun.

▼ LE BON TEMPS ROULÉ
Live Music & Neighborhood Bar
☎ 897-3448; 4801 Magazine St; ⏷ 11am-3am

This is the sort of excellent neighborhood bar where a lesbian punches a guy for trying to steal her girlfriend's Abita, and all three laugh about the incident afterwards. Come on Thursday nights to see Soul Rebels brass band tear the joint up, or Fridays for free oysters from 7pm to 10pm.

▼ MS MAE'S Dive
☎ 895-9401; 4336 Magazine St; ⏷ 24hr

Calling Ms Mae's a dive is like calling the Pacific Ocean a body of water; it's technically true, but kind of misses the spirit of the thing. How this 24-hour den of all that is sinful, grotty and fun has survived in its location right across from a police precinct remains a mystery. See if you can spot Ms Mae herself; she looks, well, exactly like a Louisiana lady who manages one of the toughest bars in the city. Be nice and she might do a shot with you.

▼ SNAKE & JAKES Dive
☎ 861-2802; www.snakeandjakes.com; 7612 Oak St; ⏷ 24hr

When you see the grey light of dawn creep under the door and hear the birds chirp their infuriating morning song of happiness at Snake & Jakes, pat yourself on the back: you, friend, are an honorary New Orleanian. It's unsigned, decked out in Christmas lights and located in what looks like a tool shed. When someone says, 'Let's go to Snakes,' that's a sure sign the night is either going to get much better, or immeasurably worse.

�☐ ST JOE'S BAR
Neighborhood Bar

☎ 899-3744; 5535 Magazine St;
🕑 5pm-late

Joe's is one of the better neighborhood bars in the city, voted 'best mojitos' by New Orleanians several times and sporting a jukebox well stocked with jazz, rock and blues. The crowd is in their 20s and 30s, friendly and chatty, as are the staff. The main draw is the layout, which, while narrow in the front, leads past a series of faux-Catholic shrines into a spacious backyard that feels like a cross between an Indonesian island and a Thai temple – a good spot for one of those aforementioned mojitos.

PLAY

★ MAPLE LEAF BAR *Live Music*

☎ 866-9359; 8316 Oak St; cover $5-10, admission free Mon; 🕑 3pm-4am

The legendary Maple Leaf is the premier nighttime destination in the Riverbend area. Its dimly lit pressed-tin caverns are the kind of environs you'd expect from a New Orleans juke joint. Scenes from the film *Angel Heart* were shot here, and on Tuesdays the Rebirth brass band hosts one of the best weekly gigs in the city.

★ TIPITINA'S *Live Music*

☎ 895-8477, concert line 897-3943; www.tipitinas.com; 501 Napoleon Ave; cover $8-25; 🕑 5pm-late

'Tips,' as locals call it, is one of New Orleans' great musical meccas. The legendary nightclub, which takes its name from Professor Longhair's 1953 hit single, is the site of some of the city's most memorable shows, particularly when big names like Dr John come home to roost. Outstanding music from the local talent pool still packs 'em in year-round, and this is one of the few non–French Quarter bars tourists regularly trek out to.

>MID-CITY & THE TREMÉ

The name alone – Mid-City – suggests a middle ground, and that is what this neighborhood is: a transition space between the disparate elements that make up New Orleans. Geographically, racially, economically, architecturally, even layout-wise, running from commercial strips to cozy blocks of residential housing, Mid-City is perhaps the most fascinating neighborhood in the city because it encompasses said city as a single unit. If that weren't reason enough to explore this side of town, how about this added incentive: it's topped by City Park, one of the prettiest parks in America. Nearby, the Tremé is the oldest African American neighborhood in the country. It can be rough, but alongside its edginess is the history and identity of the most influential ethnic group in New Orleans' history. You may be able to spot a second-line parade here; and you're sure to learn more about what makes this town unique.

MID-CITY & THE TREMÉ

Please see over for map

GETTING HERE
Bus 88 runs on Rampart St between the Tremé and the French Quarter, and connects to the Bywater along St Claude Ave. Bus 91 runs up and down Esplanade Ave from City Park to Rampart St. Bus 27 goes to City Park from the Garden District primarily via Louisiana and Washington Aves. The City Park line of the Canal St streetcar diverges from the main line at Carrollton Ave, where it turns onto N Carrollton, ending at Esplanade Ave and Bayou St John near the entrance of the New Orleans Museum of Art.

SEE

BACKSTREET CULTURAL MUSEUM
☎ 287-5224; www.backstreetmuseum .org; 1116 St Claude Ave; donations ac-cepted; 🕑 10am-5pm Tue-Sat
New Orleans has one of the most distinctive urban cultures in the world, and this museum is the place to see how one facet of its identity – its African American side (the term 'backstreet' refers to New Orleans' 'back o' town,' or the poor black neighbor-hoods) – is expressed in daily life. If you have any interest in Mardi Gras Indian suits, second-line parades etc, stop by this small but fascinating annex. Best to call ahead, as opening hours aren't consistent.

CAROUSEL GARDENS & STORYLAND
☎ 483-9382; http://neworleanscitypark .com/storyland_kids; admission $3; 🕑 10am-3pm Tue-Fri, 11am-6pm Sat & Sun
This charmingly dated park is anchored by an antique carousel, restored by residents in the 1980s into spectacular, twee, tinkly fun. Storyland has no rides, but the fairy-tale statuary is lovely. Children can climb upon the Jabberwocky from *Alice in Wonderland,* or enter the mouth of the whale from *Pinocchio.*

Going round in circles at Carousel Gardens

CITY PARK
☎ 482-4888; www.neworleanscity
park.com
Three miles long, 1 mile wide,
stroked by weeping willows and
Spanish moss and dotted with
museums, gardens, waterways,
bridges, birds and the occasional
alligator, this is the nation's fifth-
largest urban park (bigger than
Central Park in New York City) and
New Orleans' prettiest green lung.
City Park is ridiculously picturesque
and the perfect expression of a
local 'park' in the sense that it's an
only slightly tamed expression of
the Louisiana wetlands and forest
that are the natural backdrop of
the city. The arboreal life here is
magnificent: dense groves of mature live oaks – thousands of them,
some as old as 600 years – along
with bald cypresses, Southern
magnolias and other species.

FAIR GROUNDS RACE
COURSE
☎ 944-5515; www.fairgroundsrace
course.com; 1751 Gentilly Blvd
Besides placing yer bets, this is
where you can catch the New
Orleans Jazz & Heritage Festival
(p117), the second-largest event in
the city after Mardi Gras.

Sign up here to enter: the decorative, arched entrance to Louis Armstrong Park (p106)

Ted Hornick
Americorps volunteer, YURP & former editor-in-chief of The Trumpet

Why did you move to New Orleans? I moved to New Orleans in August 2007, based on my college roommate's (from Louisiana) recommendation. The same friend encouraged me to apply to work with Americorps in the rebuilding and I applied about two weeks before the deadline. **Can you describe what you were doing when you got here?** I spent 10 months working as editor-in-chief of *The Trumpet,* a non-profit community newspaper formed by the Neighborhoods Partnership Network (NPN). NPN's goal is to connect New Orleans' diverse communities in sharing resources and documenting the recovery. **How are you and other new New Orleanians changing the character of the city?** The nature of the city was pretty fragmented *before* the hurricane, in my opinion. You had a diverse population divided by lines of class, race and culture interacting and co-existing in communities that were very different. The YURPs or post-hurricane developers or whatever you want to call them have to be conscious about just how distinct New Orleans is and how important each of these groups is to the city's identity. **Where are you living?** I moved to Mid-City at the beginning of 2009 to reassess my commitment to the city and to be closer to my job. The area is close to Bayou St John (p107) and is among the most tranquil places I've lived. It's a great place to walk and read. I also enjoy a po' boy from Parkway Tavern (p109).

◉ LOUIS ARMSTRONG PARK

The bare-bulb-lit entrance to this massive park is a picturesque arch that ought rightfully be the final set piece in some Jazz Age period film. Inside, check out Congo Sq: this was where slaves were allowed to practice their music and rituals under French rule, preserving a tradition that paved the way for the development of all of New Orleans' indigenous forms of music. Be careful here at night.

◉ NEW ORLEANS MUSEUM OF ART

☎ 658-4100; www.noma.org; 1 Collins Diboll Circle; adult $8, concession $4-7; ⏱ 10am-5pm Thu-Tue, noon-8pm Wed

Looking vaguely like a cross between a library, Lenin's tomb and a Greek temple, this is one of the finest museums in the city and one of the best art museums in the entire South. There's strong representation by regional artists, but masters who have passed through the city, such as Edgar Degas, are

Elisabeth Frink's *Riace Warriors I, II, III, IV* check out the Sydney & Walda Besthoff Sculpture Garden

BORN ON THE BAYOU

Bayou St John is a dark slipstream of water that runs along the eastern edge of City Park. Once the city's primary portage, today the bayou is one of the best places in New Orleans to stroll, admire handsome Creole mansions, catch concerts on the grassy median or kayak and canoe. The Army Corps of Engineers says St John is a dangerous source of floodwater and has proposed sealing it off, but some residents say re-establishing a natural flow of water would freshen up the bayou and re-introduce important flora and fauna along its banks.

also prominent. The top-floor exhibition of Africa, Asian, Oceania, pre-Columbian and Native American art is stunning.

☉ ST LOUIS CEMETERY NO 1

admission free; ⏲ 8am-3pm
The most famous necropolis in the city opened in 1789; today, it's stuffed with graves and lotsa tourists. The supposed crypt of voodoo queen Marie Laveau is (illegally) scratched with 'XXX's and sits adjacent to the resting place of Ernest 'Dutch' Morial, New Orleans' first black mayor. The Italian Mutual Benevolent Society Tomb is the tallest monument in the cemetery. You're free to wander around on your own, but you could glean more from this spot as part of an organized walking tour.

☉ SYDNEY & WALDA BESTHOFF SCULPTURE GARDEN

☎ 488-2631; www.noma.org; 1 Collins Diboll Circle; ⏲ noon-8pm Wed, 10am-4:45pm Thu-Sun
Just outside the New Orleans Museum of Art, the Besthoff Sculpture Garden opened in 2003 with some 45 pieces from the world-renowned Besthoff collection. The garden collection is growing and includes mostly contemporary works by artists like Antoine Bourdelle, Henry Moore and Louis Bourgeois.

EAT

🍴 ANGELO BROCATO

Ice Cream $
☎ 486-1465; www.angelobrocatoice cream.com; 214 N Carrollton Ave; ⏲ 11am-5pm Tue-Sat
When an ice-cream parlor passes the 100-year mark, you gotta just step back and say, 'Alright. Clearly, they're doing something right.' This is the oldest ice-cream shop in New Orleans, and we'd come for the beautiful copper espresso machine alone, but then there's the marble-top counter, silky gelatos, perfect cannoli, crispy biscotti and irreplaceable sense of history. *Molto bene.*

DOOKY CHASE
Soul Food & Creole $
☎ 821-0600; 2301 Orleans Ave;
🕐 11am-2:30pm Tue-Fri

Ray Charles wrote 'Early in the Morning' about Dooky's, local civil rights leaders used the spot as an informal headquarters in the 1960s and Barack Obama ate here when he visited New Orleans after his inauguration. Leah Chase's labor of love is a backbone of the Tremé, serving grillades (slow-cooked meat, traditionally served with grits), fried chicken and perhaps the best meal for any vegetarian visiting New Orleans: the gumbo z'herbes. Served on Thursdays during Lent, this is the great New Orleans dish done green and gorgeous with mustards, beet tops, spinach, kale, collards and Leah knows what else – even committed carnivores should give it a try.

FAIR GRINDS *Cafe* $
☎ 913-9072; http://fairgrinds.com; 3133 Ponce de Leon St; 🕐 6:30am-10pm

Fair Grinds is simultaneously airy and comfy and hip and unpretentious, and the coffee's good to boot. It showcases local art and generally acts as the beating heart of Mid-City's bohemian scene; plus it supports, through donations and promotions, any number of community development associations.

FIVE HAPPINESS *Chinese* $
☎ 482-3935; http://fivehappiness.com; 3605 S Carrollton Ave; 🕐 11am-10pm Mon-Thu & Sun, to 11pm Fri & Sat

This unassuming spot is every locals' favorite Chinese, serving up the gluey, oily standards like pepper steak and sweet-and-sour everything you expect in any Chinese restaurant anywhere (besides China). It may not be gastronomically thrilling, but with three decades of history behind it, Five Happiness is very much a beloved landmark on the culinary landscape.

HUEVOS *Diner* $
☎ 482-6264; 4408 Banks St; 🕐 7am-3pm

'Huevos' is Spanish for eggs. Don't you love a restaurant that knows what it's good at? Really. It's eggs and eggs only, thrown into one of the most incredible enormous breakfast sandwiches in the city, poached on hash with sausage and bacon and ranchero-ed out with black beans. Try the chicory coffee, or as we like to think of it, rocket fuel.

LIL' DIZZY'S *Soul Food* $
☎ 569-8997; 1500 Esplanade Ave; 🕐 7am-2:30pm Mon-Fri, to 2pm Sat

One of the city's great lunch spots, Dizzy's does mean soul-food specials in a historic shack owned by the Baquet family. The fried chicken is excellent, the hot sausages may be better and the bread pudding is divine. Our one gripe is the gumbo, which was more like thin brown water.

🍴 LIUZZA'S BY THE TRACK
Diner $
☎ 218-7888; 1518 N Lopez St; 🕑 11am-7pm Mon-Sat
The quintessential Mid-City neighborhood joint does some of the best gumbo in town, a barbecue shrimp po'boy to die for and legendary deep-fried garlic oysters. Always start your visit with a beer and an inspection of the daily specials (red beans and rice, pork chops and the like), which are always up to scratch. We've seen former city judges and strippers dining out together in this spot, which is an experience as only-in–New Orleans as they come.

🍴 LOLA'S *Spanish* $$
☎ 488-6946; 3312 Esplanade Ave; mains $7-18; 🕑 5:30-9:30pm Sun-Thu, to 10pm Fri & Sat
Wait outside in that warm Esplanade air with clouds of Mid-City locals who swear by Lola's paellas and *fideuas* (an angel-hair pasta variation on the former). Once you get inside, it's all elbows and crowds and buzz of conversation and, incidentally, some very good grub.

This isn't haute Barcelona cuisine; it's the sort of Spanish peasant fare Hemingway wrote chapters about, all rabbit and meats and hams and fresh seafood and olive oil and lots of lots of delicious garlic – vampires need not apply.

🍴 MANDINA'S *Italian* $$
☎ 482-9179; www.mandinasrestaurant.com; 3800 Canal St; 🕑 11am-9:30pm Mon-Thu, to 10pm Fri & Sat, noon-9pm Sun
In the Italian American community in New Orleans, funerals were followed by a visit to this century-old institution for the turtle soup. That's just the way it was and that's what Mandina's is: the way it was. When you've been around for over 100 years you stick to what you know. In this case that's Sicilian-Louisiana food: trout almandine, red beans and rice with veal cutlets, and bell peppers stuffed with macaroni and meat. The family-style dining room, in its way, is as historic as any building in the city and just as crucial to its culture. Cash only.

🍴 PARKWAY TAVERN *Po'boys* $
☎ 482-3047; www.parkwaybakeryand tavernnola.com; 538 N Hagan Ave; 🕑 11am-10pm Tue-Sat
No one is going to settle the 'best po'boy in New Orleans' argument anytime soon, but tell a local you think the top sandwich comes from Parkway and you will get, at the very least, a nod of respect.

The roast beef in particular (a dying art in these parts) is messy as hell and twice as good. Take one down to nearby Bayou St John, feel the wind on the water and munch that sandwich in the shade. Louisiana bliss.

¶¶ WILLIE MAE'S SCOTCH HOUSE Soul Food $
☎ 822-9503; 2401 St Ann St; 🕙 11am-3pm Mon-Fri

Willie Mae's (and specifically, its fried chicken) was named an 'American Classic' by the James Beard foundation in 2005, eight weeks before the restaurant was swamped by Katrina. Subsequently, a huge community effort went into re-opening Willie Mae's, and the narrative of hope was irresistible. That said, we gotta admit the bird in this little white house in a low-income neighborhood, while very, very good, isn't the best fried chicken in the world, whatever the hype may claim.

Visitors wander through New Orleans' most famous necropolis, St Louis Cemetery No 1 (p107)

DRINK

ⓨ K-DOE'S MOTHER-IN-LAW
LOUNGE *Lounge*
☎ 947-1078; www.k-doe.com/lounge;
1500 N Claiborne Ave; ⏰ 5pm-late
Ernie K-Doe was famous for
writing the song 'Mother-in-Law'
and frequently proclaiming his
'Emperorship of 'he Universe.'
The Mother-in-Law lounge carries
on his surreal legacy, filled with
life-sized statutes of the Emperor of
the Universe, touching pictures of
his empress (dearly departed wife,
Antoinette) and lots of loyal customers. Note the hearse out front:
Antoinette bought it before Katrina
(because, hey, a hearse has storage
space, right?) and staff apparently
used the car to sneak back into the
flooded city several times (because
who's going to stop a hearse?).

ⓨ MID-CITY YACHT CLUB
Neighborhood Bar
☎ 483-2517; http://midcityyachtclub
.com; 440 S Patrick St; ⏰ 5pm-late
The Yacht Club, a quintessential
post-softball-game kind of pub, is
so much a part of the neighbor-

hood one of the owners took his
boat out to save flooded Katrina
victims after the storm (hence the
name of the bar, which isn't anywhere near a lake or ocean). And so
much a part of the neighborhood
the neighborhood is literally a part
of it: the bar is actually made from
wood salvaged from storm debris.

PLAY

✪ MID-CITY ROCK & BOWL
Live Music
☎ 861-1700; www.rockandbowl.com;
3000 S Carrollton Ave; ⏰ 5pm-late
A night at the Rock & Bowl is
a quintessential New Orleans
experience, but as it was in the
process of moving to 3000 S Carrollton at the time of writing, we
were not able to check out its new
gigs at its current location. Friends
who have gone say the scene and
the shows are the same as ever:
a strange, wonderful combination of bowling alley, deli, and a
huge live music and dance venue,
where patrons get down to New
Orleans roots music while trying
to avoid that 7-10 split.

New Orleans is all about sensory overload: spicy taste of hot sauce, muddy smell of marsh, crashing groove of brass band, grainy wood in antique stores and a torch flicker-lighting the street. Here's where to find more shades of local color.

Ann St house displaying the French Quarter's distinctive residential architecture

SNAPSHOTS > ACCOMMODATIONS

ACCOMMODATIONS

Traveler, you are in a city that enjoys its indulgences, and you will be treated royally by the staff of this city's greatest hotels. There is a real sense of age and tradition to the city's lodging, but with plenty of modern amenities as well. The digs tend to run the gamut from elegant old mansions converted into B&Bs to conventioneer land downtown to sleek, chic hotels.

Where you stay in New Orleans depends on why you've come. Plan to play the whole time in the French Quarter? Your best bet is shelling out the few extra bucks to stay there. You can't beat having all the food and fun at your doorstep – and you can save the cost of taxis or a rental car. Small hotels and inns are the hallmark of this historic district. Choose a room with a streetside balcony and you can watch the revelry in your pajamas; courtyard views are a bit quieter. But the Quarter is not all booze and Bourbon St; there are calmer residential corners to the northwest and northeast where you can enjoy this area's distinctive architecture without ever having to deal with the booze-geois of Middle America just a few blocks away.

Looking for a more local experience? Northeast of Esplanade Ave, the Quarter morphs into Faubourg Marigny, an arty, transitional neighborhood with quirky B&Bs and great nightlife. There is a fair bit of gay-friendly lodging in this part of town as well. Further afield, public transportation puts the Lower and Upper Garden Districts' B&Bs and moderate lodgings in easy reach. The leafy lanes here ooze a gentrified quiet near the city's best shopping on Magazine St, just a few blocks away. Continue west along St Charles Ave to Uptown and Riverbend, where mansions host glorious inn-like guesthouses close to Tulane University.

 Hotels & Hostels

Need a place to stay? Find and book it at lonelyplanet.com. More than 100 properties are featured for New Orleans – each personally visited, thoroughly reviewed and happily recommended by a Lonely Planet author. From hostels to high-end hotels, we've hunted out the places that will bring you unique and special experiences. Read independent reviews by authors and other travelers, and get practical information including amenities, maps and photos. Then reserve your room simply and securely via our online booking service. It's all at www.lonelyplanet.com/hotels.

Need to seal a deal? Mammoth business hotels and conference centers populate the CBD and Warehouse District. Prices here drop to surprising lows on weekends and when convention business is slow. The options around Canal St border the Quarter, but don't expect intimate accommodation or character-filled cottages – this is where you'll find chain big box high-rise hotels. That said, you will be as centrally located as possible.

Those arriving for Jazz Fest should book at one of the few mansion–turned–B&Bs on Esplanade Ridge in Mid-City. These are some of the most distinctive and soulful sleeping options in town. You'll need a cab to get to the Quarter, but you can hoof it to the sounds of the big show. If you're trying to book a room here close to any sort of big festival or event, make sure to reserve as far in advance as possible.

For more information, check out www.neworleanshotels.com and www.neworleansfinehotels.com. You'll usually find cheaper bookings and deals by reserving a room online. A list of B&Bs can be found at www.experienceneworleans.com/bandbs.

CHEAP & CHEERFUL
> India House Hostel (www.indiahouse hostel.com)
> St Peter House Hotel (www.stpeter house.com)
> Frenchmen Hotel (www.frenchmen hotel.com)
> Bywater Bed & Breakfast (www.by waterbnb.com)
> St James Hotel (www.neworleans finehotels.com)

MODERN & MOD-ISH
> W French Quarter (www.whotels.com)
> Loft 523 (www.loft523.com)
> Westin New Orleans at Canal Place (www.westin.com)
> W New Orleans (www.whotels.com)
> International House (www.ih hotel.com)

GAY STAYS
> W Hotels (www.whotels.com)
> Green House Inn (www.thegreen houseinn.com)
> Magnolia Mansion (www.magnolia mansion.com)
> Bywater Bed & Breakfast (www.by waterbnb.com)
> Biscuit Palace Guest House (www.biscuitpalace.com)

CREOLE CLASSICS
> House on Bayou Road (www.houseon bayouroad.com)
> Lagniappe Bed & Breakfast (www.lanyappe.com)
> Hotel Maison de Ville & Audubon Cottages (www.hotelmaisondeville.com)
> Sweet Olive Bed & Breakfast (www.sweetolive.com)
> Degas House (www.degashouse.com)

FESTIVALS

A multicultural city that fairly drips with history has invented (or helped invent) several of America's greatest genres of music and cuisine and lives off tourism? Er, yeah. New Orleans is, if anything, a city of festivals. To be honest, it starts wearing on you if you live here: c'mon Nola, give us a weekend without some kind of celebration, already…

No? Oh, alright then. When you think about it, residents have no right to complain about the festive nature of this town. First of all, it makes New Orleans a hell of a lot of fun to live in. And second, it gives the casual visitor unparalleled access to what makes this city tick. We love the museums here, but nothing helps you learn about this city like participating in the parades, concerts and generally festival-y *lagniappe* (extras) that are crucial to the city's self-perception. Late spring and early summer, when the weather is at its most pleasant, is prime festival season in the city.

Of course, February's **Mardi Gras** (www.mardigras.com) is the festival everyone associates with this city. It's so integral to the New Orleans image it almost transcends the word festival; we can't imagine any other event that is as iconic to a city's identity as Mardi Gras is to New Orleans. Books and dissertations have been written about the complicated history and cultural practices of this event and the way they shape New Orleans.

Just barely behind in import is one of the world's great music events: **Jazz Fest** (www.nojazzfest.com). Since hosting 350 people in 1970, Jazz Fest has grown into the kind of event that pulls in hundreds of thousands of concert-goers, internationally known names like Ben Harper, Bon Jovi and Wynton Marsalis, and the local talent that makes this one of the most musically rich cities in America: Mardi Gras Indians, Theresa Andersson, Soul Rebels brass band and Dr John. It goes down over a period of two weeks in late April and early May, and is catered by some of the best restaurants in the city. If you don't want to shell out $50 a day for Jazz Fest, why not opt for the much more low key and casually fun **Chaz Fest** (www.chazfestival.com), held around the same time, which features those New Orleans artists who don't make it into the increasingly crowded Jazz Fest line-up.

The **French Quarter Festival** (www.fqfi.org), held in April, consistently show-cases a good range of local music and local food, although honestly, we could use this description for every festival we describe here. The focus, obviously, is on displaying the finest of the Quarter, and this is one of the best times to stroll those narrow streets; many private residences throw their beautiful courtyard gardens open to visitors at this time.

St Patrick's Day is celebrated with a lot of passion here; the biggest events go down at Irish American bars like Molly's (p49) and Parasol's (p82). **Indian Sunday** (www.mardigrasindians.com) is held on March 19; this is one of the best times of year to see the famous tribes in all their regalia. The **Wine & Food Experience** (www.nowfe.com) in May is clearly a good bet for foodies, who may also appreciate the **Louisiana Crawfish Festival** (www.louisianacrawfish festival.com) in late March/early April.

The **Essence Music Festival** (www.essence.com/essence/emf) in July packs in some of the best R&B and hip-hop talent in the country, while July 4 itself is celebrated with huge fireworks displays over the Mississippi River. On August 4, Louis Armstrong's birthday is celebrated with jazz and food (natch) at **Satchmo SummerFest** (www.fqfi.com/satchmosummerfest), and the **Southern Decadence party** (www.southerndecadence.com) on Labor Day weekend (preced-ing the first Monday in September), also known as 'Gay Mardi Gras,' keeps the entire city partying into the wee hours. Halloween is huge in the city that loves to throw on a mask, while Christmas features numerous fiery festivals along the waterfront, including **Celebration in the Oaks** (http://celebration intheoaks.com), when the colorful lights are thrown up in City Park.

Top left A saxophonist plays it cool at the New Orleans Mardi Gras

SNAPSHOTS

FOOD

Louisiana may have the greatest native culinary tradition in the USA – not necessarily because of the quality of food (although quality is very high) but the long history behind dishes that are older than most American states. Also, people here just *love to eat*. Yes, New York, London and Melbourne have their dedicated foodie contingents, but let's be honest: it's a bit of a yuppie thing, even when it comes to eating cheap. New Orleans' love of food is beautifully democratic: everyone in this city, from Garden District mansion-dwellers to St Roch tenement-residents, goes crazy when fecal-eating, sewage-dwelling mudbugs come into season (crawfish, y'all).

'Craws' represent one facet of the goodness of Louisiana food: the incredible bounty of the Mississippi delta. The other ingredients are the culinary creativity of cultures that have settled here and, standing somewhat in opposition, the slow construction of tradition. See, a debate among many chefs in America is hybridization versus loyalty to regional influence. Louisiana in general, but New Orleans in particular, manages to bring these two seemingly disparate philosophies together into delicious matrimony. In this great, old multiculti port, Creole-ization – mixing it all up – *is* the tradition. Think of a place like Patois (p96), which literally means 'accent.' Here, the old-school French 'accent' is seamlessly blended with traces of local flavor, like a red wine and ham hock reduction poured over grilled rib eye.

It's not all subtle creativity, though. Another defining feature of New Orleans food is an in-grown disregard, if not contempt, for moderation and that, ultimately, is what makes the food here so fun. Think of that bacon you had with the brown sugar, or the cheese and gravy sliding off a shrimp po'boy, or wild boar pâté with watermelon pickles at John Besh's Luke (p71).

There's also some big celebrity chef presence here: Susan Spicer at Bayona (p46), Donald Link at Cochon (p70) and, of course, Emeril Lagasse BAMing it up in no less than three restaurants (see Emeril's, p70) – the list goes on. Spicer, in particular, actually works *in* her kitchen and may have a hand in cooking your food, which is more than we can say for big-name chefs in many other parts of America. Lots of young cooks are coming here, too, bringing sharp kitchen knives and a sharper sense of ambition to a town with a big food presence and less rent and competition than, say, San Francisco.

Back to the food, though…because hey, it's the food that matters. And food *matters* here. It's inextricably tied up in sense of place, and few cities in America emanate such a distinctive sense of place as New Orleans. This city finds itself in its food; meals are both an expression of identity and bridges between white and black and brown and native and transplant and rich and poor. To balance the loud demands of pride and tradition, the settlers of this city – Acadians, Germans, Irish, Jews, Africans and Vietnamese – have added their ingredients to (yes, we'll say it, cliché it may be) the New Orleans gumbo. Said soup takes new influences in and spits them out: if not gentrified, at least Creole-ed up.

It comes down to this: New Orleans is inhabited by cultures drawn from gastronomic Europe (Spain, France and Sicily), soul food–loving black America and Southeast Asia (Vietnamese refugees). The greatest food cultures in the world are here, given license to let loose by American prosperity and love of huge portions and doing things like stuffing a chicken into a duck into a turkey (Louisiana invented the 'turkducken,' the beast described above). Throw some bacon on the side (what the hell) and the baby of this gastronomic holy matrimony is a food culture that is obsessed with serving rich food until your mind melts, but that's OK, because why live after eating here?

BEST FOR UNDER $20
> Boucherie (p92)
> Dooky Chase (p108)
> The Joint (p59)
> Stein's Deli (p83)
> Fiorella's (p47)

BEST HIGH-END CREOLE & SOUTHERN
> Mat and Naddie's (p96)
> Elizabeth's (p58)
> Cochon (p70)
> Brigtsen's Restaurant (p93)
> Bayona (p46)

Above Shrimp, crawfish and oysters in a superb seafood gumbo

BARS

New Orleans is a city that loves life, including nightlife, and it has some of the finest bars around. The scene runs the gamut from great dives to posh watering holes of the 'thumpa-thumpa-thumpa' music and everyone-dressed-to-impress variety. The one commonality New Orleans watering holes possess is a genuine conviviality. This is, straight up, a friendly town for a drink, and a drink is always in order, even in the middle of the work day (a phenomenon that's kind of rare in other American towns). Most New Orleans bars also have great outdoor gardens, perfect for al fresco ambience (or annihilation, depending on what kind of mood you're in).

The New Orleans dive is a little rough, but rarely surly. They're dirty, of course, but that's what you're paying for, and you're not paying much. Prices are incredibly cheap compared to the rest of the USA – where but at Ms Mae's (p98) can you find a beer and a shot for $3? Posher drinks are found mainly in the city center and the swankier environs of the French Quarter. You can't go wrong in spots like Le Phare Bar (p72) and Whiskey Blue (p72) if you're looking for dim lighting and sexy dressing (although this being New Orleans, such dressing may consist of the perpetually nerdy seersucker ensemble). These are the sort of lounges where every-one looks like they should be in a hip-hop video doing a line-up freak dance around you every time you enter the door.

For a more refined, Old World-ish tipple, try swanky hotel bars like Carousel (p49). But our favorite high-end bars in New Orleans eschew an atmosphere of exclusivity while still serving top-quality drinks. Both Tonique (p49) and Cure (p98) produce expertly mixed cocktails – a type of drink this city claimed to *invent,* so you know they take 'em seriously – that will lay you flat both in terms of quality and the strength of the drink itself. As fancy as some places may seem in terms of sleek decor, we never once felt any attitude while visiting them. That's just not the New Orleans way.

But the best New Orleans bar falls between dive and diva, and manifests as the excellent, oft-attended neighborhood bars. These aren't quite pubs – the weather's too warm for the fireplace-centered, heavy-pint-pouring British institution – but the vibe is about the same. They are places where everyone knows your name and if they don't, they'll soon learn it. On weekends, many of these humble 'hood watering holes transform into buzzing hotspots for picking up and getting smashed with friends. Visit bars like the Bridge Lounge (p84) for a sense of the above; it evolves over the week from a place to take your dog into a haunt for hotties and hangers-on. Bars like St Joe's (p99), with its Christian iconography and Balinese backyard, would be jammed with sneering scenesters in other towns; here, Joe's hosts regulars, the occasional tourist, and is the heart of the local community.

There is a shadow to New Orleans' sunny drinking scene. The tourist bars on Bourbon St and the immediate vicinity are fun if you're feeling rowdy, but in general, they replace the city's standard cheerful energy with a more aggressive frat boy attitude. There's also a fair bit of racial segregation in New Orleans' bars. While you'll find black customers in predominately white bars, the reverse is rarely true. Even copious booze can't wash away all of the city's social divides.

BEST BAR GARDENS
> Bacchanal (p58)
> Tonique (p49)
> Maple Leaf (p99)
> Bulldog (p84)
> Saint (p84)

SINGLES SCENE
> Yuki Izakaya (p60)
> Bridge Lounge (p84)
> R Bar (p60)
> Le Phare Bar (p72)
> Balcony Bar (p84)

Top left Always a spot for a drink in one of New Orleans' many neighborhood watering holes

LIVE MUSIC

We'll open this snapshot by pointing out the one genre of music venue New Orleans lacks: the big box mega club. As much as people in this city love both noise and getting their groove on, huge club spaces simply aren't their thing.

That doesn't mean live music isn't. It can easily be argued the act of watching a good gig is more integral to New Orleans nightlife than it is in any other city in America. Going out, drinking, dancing and listening to a band simply go very much hand in hand here. It's a rare night when these activities are segregated into different portions of the evening; one pretty much always follows into the other. The best listings in the city can be found at www.nolafunguide.com and www.bestofneworleans.com.

The city's history can be traced in its music. The French and their descendants, the Creoles, were mad about ballroom dancing and opera. New Orleans boasted two opera companies before any other American city had even one. Meanwhile, slaves and free people of color preserved African music and dance at public markets such as Congo Sq. These European and African influences inevitably came together when French-speaking black Creoles, who prided themselves on their musicianship and training, began livening up traditional European dance tunes by adding African rhythms. From there, jazz was inevitable. While Katrina scattered many of the city's musicians, the recent return of great talents and names from big ticket cities like New York speaks to the loyalty and solidarity many homegrown musicians feel for their town.

One reason we love New Orleans with such undying affection is the fact you can go out and catch regular shows, often accompanied by free (or at least very cheap) food, every night of the week. See p32 for a list of shows, to which we'd add Mr Quintron, a keyboardist/inventor who kind of lives in his own galaxy. He often performs with his wife, underground puppeteer (just see it) Miss Pussycat, at the **Spellcaster Lodge** (www .quintronandmisspussycat.com; 3052 St Claude Ave) in the Bywater neighborhood.

BEST LIVE DIVES
> Circle Bar (p71)
> Saturn Bar (p61)
> Le Bon Temps Roulé (p98)
> Hi Ho (p59)
> Vaughan's (p61)

FAVORITE JAZZ SPOTS
> Snug Harbor (p61)
> Preservation Hall (p51)
> Donna's Bar & Grill (p50)
> d.b.a. (p61)
> Maple Leaf Bar (p99)

Top left Keeping traditional jazz alive at Preservation Hall (p51) **Above** Squeezing out zydeco in the French Quarter

SNAPSHOTS

SHOPPING

It's easy to assume that the shopping scene in New Orleans primarily consists of cheap souvenirs, with a decided focus on Mardi Gras beads. But beyond tourist tat, there's a consumer character to this town that's about vintage beauty and antique nostalgia. In the French Quarter, near Royal St, you'll find a glut of cute antique and curio stores that encompasses this, such as the sweet-smelling old-school scents on sale in Hové Parfumeur (p45) and the dusty atlases in Centuries (p44). New Orleans is also a city that rewards those seeking out oddball finds and eccentricities. Note, for example, the glut of 'outsider' folk art galleries, such as the excellent Anton Haardt Gallery (p78) in the Garden District.

This town lends itself to finding the perfect individualized gift for a loved one, be they family member, friend or special someone. Try getting them something from charming bookstores like Faulkner House (p44) if you're near Jackson Sq. Or if you know someone who's into the undead, how about some spells from Boutique du Vampyre (p44)?

Head a little north into Faubourg Marigny and the Bywater for art studios and supply shops, plus a few tattoo parlors for good measure. If you're downtown, you can browse the art galleries near Julia St, or just hit up the **Shops at Canal Place** (Map pp64-5; ☎ 522-9200; www.theshopsatcanalplace .com; 333 Canal St) or **Riverwalk Marketplace** (Map pp64-5; ☎ 522-1555; www.riverwalk marketplace.com; 1 Poydras St) for chain-Americana retail therapy. But if you're really serious about doing some hardcore shopping, for your guy, girl or yourself, undoubtedly the best strip in the city is Magazine St, which curves like a smiling beacon of consumerism along the bottom of New Orleans' river-cut 'U.'

Be you metrosexual guy in need of cufflinks and an expensive shave at Aidan Gill (p78), Tulane co-ed in need of a new summer frock at Sweet Pea & Tulip (p92) or aspiring artist on trust fund requiring some atmospheric period furniture (about any store within tripping distance), Magazine has got you covered.

BEST SHOPPING STREETS
> Magazine St
> S Carrollton Ave, riverside
> Royal St
> Chartres St
> Decatur St

SHOP LOCAL!
> Meyer the Hatter (p68)
> Green Project (p56)
> Shoefty (p92)
> Yvonne Lefleur (p92)
> Anything off www.staylocal.org

TOP NEW ORLEANS FASHION ITEMS
> A 'Defend New Orleans' T-shirt (any clothing store)
> Unique vintage jewelry from Trashy Diva (p80)
> Snazzy white khaki pants or shorts from Style Lab for Men (p80)
> A sundress from Pied Nu (p91)
> A 'y@t' sticker or similar 'only in New Orleans' in-joke accessory from Dirty Coast (p91)

Top left Undergarment glamour at Trashy Diva (p80) **Above** The Shops at Canal Place for retail therapy on demand

OUTDOORS

New Orleans is one of the greenest cities in America. We don't necessarily mean that in the progressive, environmental sense of the word 'green,' although this city is making very admirable strides in that direction as well. But New Orleans is also a very lush, overgrown town.

Some of the most quintessentially New Orleans moments the visitor can experience are inevitably wrapped up in the plants that seem to constantly be struggling to wrap this town in a shroud of green. Think of catching shade under the massive trees lining St Charles Ave in the Garden District, or watching water pool into sensual little lines down the folded, soft skin of elephant ear leaves or enjoying the lush gardens that explode out of the smallest shotgun shack yard. There are times when the sheer fecundity of New Orleans makes it feel more like Southeast Asia than the American Southeast. Indeed, those parts of the city worst hit by Hurricane Katrina do not appear ruined so much as, well, grown over. What was wiped away by the water was soon overrun by nature, so those parts of the lower Ninth Ward adjacent to the water are, in their way, beautiful: all green and brambly and bushy, if abandoned.

You can credit the unique environment of southern Louisiana – a liquid/land hybrid of slow bayous, thick wetlands, still water and black creeks – and the salt-fresh estuarine lifeblood that permeates the city and its surrounds, for the wild, almost shaggy nature of New Orleans. This extremely delicate ecosystem conceals an enormous power as well. Screw with it too much and the results – erosion and flooding – are only too obviously devastating. The way nature creeps into the standard New Orleans cityscape is not just a visual phenomenon; more than most urban areas, this is a town whose fate and future are inextricably tied to her unique geography. The best places for experiencing this geography are in Mid-City, where City Park (p104) and Bayou St John (p107) are so bucolic it feels like you've escaped to the Cajun countryside.

BEST OUTDOOR EXPERIENCES
> Lazy daze on Bayou St John (p107)
> Watching the Mississippi River from a levee (p90)
> Frisbee on Audubon Park (p90)
> Jogging through the Garden District (p74)
> Exploring City Park (p104)

WEB RESOURCES
> Louisiana Outdoors (www.nola.com /outdoors)
> Louisiana Coastal Wetlands Blog (www.louisianacoastalwetlands.com)
> Louisiana Department of Wildlife & Fisheries (www.wlf.louisiana.gov)
> New Orleans Bicycle Club (www .neworleansbicycleclub.org)
> New Orleans Recreation Department (www.cityofno.com)

Top left A still stretch of Louisiana bayou **Above** Horsing around in City Park (p104)

ARTS

The arts in New Orleans are in a transition phase. On the one hand, painters, musicians, authors and similar folk were among the thousands who fled the city following Hurricane Katrina, and some among their number did not come home. But the creative class by its nature bucks convention, and many of the city's artists were among the first back when the floodwaters receded. For more insights, see our Arts Council interview (p69).

An increased sense of civic engagement and responsibility in post-Katrina New Orleans has reinforced an atmosphere of solidarity among Nola's creative types, and sometimes it feels like you can't walk in parts of the Marigny or the Bywater without tripping on a studio or arts supply store. Institutions like the New Orleans Center for Creative Arts (Nocca; p55) are more evidence of a coming together of artists, in Nocca's case for the purpose of facilitating arts education.

This is a city whose aesthetic shifts between the fresh and hip, the classic and old school and the slightly mad outsider – often realized in folk art that playfully mixes media and found objects, creating art for the city from materials often sourced *from* the city. There's a great museum scene as well; the New Orleans Museum of Art (p106) is an underrated gem where you can happily spend a day dilly-dallying amid the galleries, while the Ogden Museum of Southern Art (p67) is a regional treasure.

Beginning in 2008, New Orleans began hosting **Prospect.1** (www.prospect-neworleans.org), currently the largest biennial contemporary arts event in the USA. Artists from around the world (and New Orleans, of course) utilized some 100,000 sq ft of gallery and public performance space for a period of two months. If you're here in the winter, you'll see New Orleans transform into one of the world's great urban-art spaces, so hurry up and book that ticket.

Schools of art here do share one important commonality. Creativity rarely seems to be done for its own sake. From the most respected museums to experimental studio spaces along St Claude Ave, there's a general sensibility among New Orleans artists that their work has a purpose: namely, keeping this weird and wonderful city alive so it can share its vision with and inspire future generations.

WEEKLY ARTS EVENTS

> New Orleans Arts District Art Walk (www.neworleansartsdistrict.com)
> Freret Street Market (www.freret market.org)
> St Claude Arts District Gallery Openings (www.scadnola.com)
> Bywater Art Market (www.art -restoration.com/bam)
> Art Market of New Orleans (www .artscouncilofneworleans.org)

ARTS INFORMATION

> Arts Council of New Orleans (www .artscouncilofneworleans.com)
> New Orleans Arts District (www .neworleansartsdistrict.com)
> ART New Orleans (www.artneworleans mag.com)
> NOLA Rising (http://nolarising.blog spot.com)
> Nolaphile (www.nolaphile.com)

PUBLIC ARTS SPACES

> New Orleans Museum of Art (p106)
> Ashé Cultural Arts Center (p85)
> Contemporary Arts Center (p66)
> Zeitgeist (p85)
> The Ogden Museum of Southern Art (p67)

DIY: SEE PUBLIC ART

> Painter painting over sunflowers, by Banksy (Clio & Carondelet Sts)
> *Rising Landscape*, by Barry Bailey (Camp & Melpomene Sts)
> Martin Luther King murals, by Bruce 'Skahor' White (near Martin Luther King & Oretha Castle-Haley Blvd)
> *House of the Rising Sun*, by Paul Deo (St Bernard NORD Center, 1500 Lafreniere St)
> Anything off www.nolagraffiti.com

Top left The Ogden Museum of Southern Art (p67) is a treasure-house of art and craft from the region

LITERARY NEW ORLEANS

They say every American author of any worth has to do a stint in New York, but we'd suggest that a short stay in the Crescent City is just as crucial. We're not alone in this assertion, either. William Faulkner, Tennessee Williams, Truman Capote, F Scott Fitzgerald, John Dos Passos, Kate Chopin, David Simon and Harry Crewes, to name a few, have all done their time here, living the lives that lend themselves to great literature.

That's the gist of it. See, great writers need to surround themselves with great stories, and New Orleans simply never stops throwing the stories at you. Every ingredient of urban inspiration is present: good food, fast men and women, crime, corruption, natural beauty, divisions, diversity, class conflict, community coming together, new immigrants, old boys clubs, alligators (alligators are always cool), slow ceiling fans, music and veritable rivers of alcohol to soothe the muse.

Ironically, though, for all the great books New Orleans has produced, it's been argued by no less than the *Oxford American* (sort of the *New Yorker* of the South…or maybe the *New Yorker* is the *Oxford American* of the North?) that there is no great New Orleans novel, which is to say a work of words that causes immediate word association upon mentioning the city or vice versa.

We'd say there are some very strong arguments against this position. *A Streetcar Named Desire* (1947), written by Tennessee Williams, has spawned a literary festival where wannabe Brandos yell 'Stella' at the sky and a *Simpsons* parody that includes one of the best songs ever written about New Orleans ('If you want to go to hell/you should make that trip/ To the Sodom and Gomorrah on the Mississipp'). *Confederacy of Dunces* (1980), by John Kennedy Toole, may be oversold as the definitive work of the city, yet it's impossible to underestimate the accuracy with which it describes the city's eccentricities.

While it may be a period piece, Robert Penn Warren's *All the King's Men* (1946), which won a Pulitzer for portraying Louisiana in the era of Governor Huey Long, is also an excellent introduction to the, shall we say, colorful world of local and state politics.

Walker Percy's first novel, *The Moviegoer* (1961), is an existentialist portrayal of a young New Orleans stockbroker, Binx Bolling, whose despair and relationship with his cousin Kate are revealed against a muted Mardi Gras background. Georgia-native Harry Crewes chose New Orleans as the backdrop for his brilliantly crafted novel, *The Knockout Artist* (1987), about a washed-up boxer who entertains at Uptown parties by knocking himself out.

Kate Chopin's *The Awakening* (1899) masterfully portrays the static oppression of a woman of her time and the culture clash between American and old-line Creole society. Ironically, this book about the suppression of a woman's voice was criticized and even banned on 'moral' grounds, but it remains one of the most piercing accounts of upper-class Creole society ever written. George Washington Cable's (1844–1925) fictional *Old Creole Days* (1879) and *The Grandissimes* (1880), and his essay *The Negro Question* (1890), are almost prescient in their observations of racial injustice and make compelling arguments for civil rights.

Hurricane Katrina practically produced its own genre of literature, primarily journalism work that focuses on the disaster and rebuilding process. *Breach of Faith* (2006), by *Times-Picayune* metro editor Jed Horne, may be the definitive work on the human error inbuilt into New Orleans' levees and relief and infrastructure networks, error that evolved into one of the USA's worst disasters. *1 Dead in Attic* (2006), by Chris Rose, another *Times-Picayune* staffer, brings humanity to the city's suffering, while *Nine Lives* (2009), by Dan Baum, is an almost epic retelling of, well, nine lives and their fates before and following the storm. In the world of TV literature, in 2009 David Simon began filming the highly anticipated *Tremé,* a series on what it means to lose – and come – home.

Top left What's in a name? The Faulkner House Bookstore (p44) used to be the premises of William Faulkner's rooms

REBUILDING NEW ORLEANS

You see them everywhere, especially in areas like Uptown, Mid-City, Faubourg Marigny, the Bywater and the Lower Garden District. They're young, idealistic and ambitious. It's sort of like the Civil Rights freedom summer movement all over again, except the new arrivals aren't just from outside. They're Northeastern, Midwestern, West Coasters and, in many cases, Southern to the bone. These are the YURPs: Young, Urban Rebuilding Professionals, the newest face of the new New Orleans.

They've entered an American city that is open to every method available of rebuilding itself. In the hard streets north of the Bywater, public arts spaces like KKProjects (p54) beautify communities, while projects like Musicians' Village (p54) create communities from concrete lots and weed-clogged land. Folks in both areas can shop at stores like the Green Project (p56), where they can refurbish homes with recyclable and salvaged building materials.

In the famous Lower Ninth Ward, Brad Pitt has been plopping the environmentally friendly homes funded by his **Make It Right foundation** (www.makeitrightnola.org), even if they do look a little out of place. In Gentilly, once one of the demographically mixed neighborhoods in the city, residents can trade in old deeds to their houses for new homes built by **Project Home Again** (www.projecthomeagain.net), funded by Barnes and Noble founder Leonard Riggio.

'Home' is the operative word in this town. Home is what people lost and are trying to reclaim. Home is what the YURPs are trying to rebuild and, as children of a generation with fewer ties to place than previous ones, perhaps rediscover. Home is why folks braved 100°F-plus weather and slopped out trash, rubble and corpses from their houses, and mowed each other's lawns and planted gardens where the lawns had been washed away. Home is why they fixed each other's roofs, sometimes using discarded pieces of swept-away flooring, and celebrated small victories with what beer they could scrape together. Those impromptu parties became their own building blocks of reconstruction, the cultural component of rebirth in a city where enjoying life is as integral as cement to keeping communities together, and creating, on every level, Home.

GREEN NEW ORLEANS
> Parkway Partners (www.parkwaypartnersnola.org) Urban gardens.
> Gulf Restoration Network (www.healthygulf.org) Coastal and wetland restoration.
> Levees.org (http://levves.org) Flood protection.
> Bush-Clinton Katrina Fund (www.bushclintonkatrinafund.org) Grants for restoration and rebuilding work.
> New Orleans Public Libraries (http://nutrias.org) Crucial to the city's future.

THINKING OF MOVING HERE?
> 504ward (www.504ward.com) Professional networking.
> Teach For America (www.teachforamerica.org)
> NolaYURP (www.nolayurp.org) For the rebuilder in all of us.
> Neighborhood Partnerships Network (www.npnnola.com) Organizing organizers.
> Americorps (www.americorps.gov) Volunteer in New Orleans through the federal government.

Top left Volunteers at Habitat for Humanity (p148) use copious amounts of elbow grease to rebuild New Orleans

V

SNAPSHOTS

ARCHITECTURE

New Orleans has the highest concentration of heritage architecture in the USA. On a very simplified level, New Orleans building styles can be divided into two schools: Creole and American. Creole buildings can be found in the French Quarter, Esplanade Ridge, Mid-City, Faubourg Marigny, the Bywater and the Tremé.

Creole structures tend to be smaller, reflecting a European focus on urban compactness and a tropical-Caribbean design that allows for space in the form of large backyard gardens (a convention that can be traced back to North African influences on Spanish and French architecture). Signature buildings of this style include townhouses encased in wrought-iron balconies on the upper floors – a way of blurring the space between the public street and the private home – and single-story Creole Cottages with steeply pitched roofs. Wood, brick and especially stucco are popular building materials. The best concentration of Creole townhouses and cottages are in the French Quarter and Faubourg Marigny, while larger Creole mansions line Bayou St John and the length of Esplanade Ave.

Larger American mansions lifted from the columned, plantation school of design run along St Charles Ave from the Garden District into Uptown (indeed, parts of Uptown were once plantations that eventually folded into the city). The shotgun shack, a house with no hallway (rooms open into each other), is the Southern American equivalent of the Northeast-ern rowhouse, and some of the best in the country cluster in the Bywater and the Irish Channel, south of the Lower Garden District.

A gorgeous wrought-iron balcony frames these apartments in the French Quarter

NEW ORLEANS FOR KIDS

New Orleans is a playground. It's represented by jesters and clowns, brightly colored beads and parades, and illuminated by torch flames and firefly blinks. Nature creeps through the stiffest Garden District walls, and alligators and other creatures from fairy tales prowl the water. Everything is bright and overly colorful and loud. It's a city that laughs longer and cries with more passion than just about anywhere else in America. It's a town deeply in touch with childhood.

As such, both kids and adults who want to act like kids – who need to go back to a time when discovery was constant and imagination could be indulged with no sense of self-consciousness – are well served in New Orleans. Be it the city's excellent park spaces, the public pageantry of Mardi Gras or the inhibition-dropping fun of a concert (and there's always a concert going on), there's just something in the sticky air that keeps New Orleanians in a state of constant play. And play, after all, is the default setting of childhood. For practical recommendations on what to do with your kids, see the following lists and check out www.bigeasy .com/kids and www.experienceneworleans.com/neworleanskids.

TAKE YOUR WEE ONES TO...
> Carousel Gardens & Storyland (p101)
> Audubon Zoo (p87)
> Louisiana Children's Museum (p66)
> Aquarium of the Americas (p63)
> Blaine Kern's Mardi Gras World (p67)

INDULGE YOUR INNER CHILD
> Spook yourself in St Louis Cemetery No 1 (p107)
> Eat bacon any time of day at Cochon (p70)
> Marvel at outsider art in the Anton Haardt Gallery (p78)
> Dance in bare feet to a zydeco concert on Bayou St John (p107)
> Dress up at Maskarade (p46)

SPORTS

This city is laid-back about everything and enjoys its indulgences, which may lead the casual observer to assume it's not into athletics. Well, this is still the South, and sports decidedly matter. It helps that game day is a force for social cohesion in a city where racial divides are real and the rebuilding process is ongoing.

The **Saints** (www.neworleanssaints.com) are the local NFL franchise, and while they've yet to win a conference championship game, let alone a Superbowl (as of 2008), folks here decidedly bleed gold and black. Game day equals massive gridlock and clogging around the home dome **Superdome** (☎ 587-3663; www.superdome.com; Sugar Bowl Dr).

If any organization in town can claim more influence than the Saints, it's the **Hornets** (www.nba.com/hornets), New Orleans' professional basketball outfit. The team was relocated to Oklahoma City following Katrina, but came home for the 2007–08 season, selling out 12 of its last 17 regular season home games. Although the Hornets have disappointed during playoffs, you gotta love the 'Fan Up' T-shirts and 'Fleur de Bee' logos that are ubiquitous across town. The team played in **New Orleans Arena** (☎ 587-3822; www.neworleansarena.com; 1501 Girod St). Both the Saints and Hornets are big all along the Gulf Coast.

As popular as professional sports are, college teams, especially the LSU Tigers ('Geaux Tigers' is seen everywhere), attract huge loyalty, even if they're based out of Baton Rouge. There's a strong (if very local in its significance) rivalry between clubs at Tulane and the University of New Orleans.

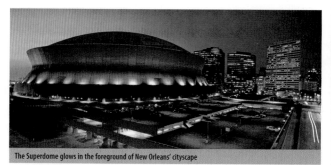

The Superdome glows in the foreground of New Orleans' cityscape

THEATER

This is a city that practically defines itself through the act of masquerade and a general love of both spectacle and the absurd. Deep French roots stretch all the way back to European stagecraft, and in general, this is a good town for drama-philes.

Tennessee Williams remains da man when it comes to historic New Orleans theater. While living at 632 St Peter St, Williams (1911–83) wrote *A Streetcar Named Desire* (1947), which portrayed Blanche Dubois' descent from elite plantation existence to life with her sister and lowbrow brother-in-law, Stanley Kowalski. As Williams descended along a path of alcohol and drug abuse, his pathos became increasingly evident in works like *Suddenly Last Summer* (1956), set against a decidedly decadent New Orleans background.

Today small companies define the local scene and perform in spaces like Le Petit Théâtre du Vieux Carré (p50), the Southern Repertory Theater (p73), which stages its productions at the Shops at Canal Place, and independent arts spaces like Zeitgeist (p85) and the Ashé Cultural Arts Center (p85).

Good shows go off at Tulane and the University of New Orleans, and independent companies pop up with increasing regularity; check the *Gambit* (www.bestofneworleans.com) or www.nolafunguide.com for listings. The historic Saenger Theater was badly water damaged by Hurricane Katrina; renovators hope to have this heritage building open to the public in time for the 2010–11 season. If you're around town in November, the **New Orleans Fringe Theater Festival** (www.nofringe.org) pushes theatrical limits in an eminently enjoyable way; it's a can't-miss.

Community theater Le Petit Théâtre du Vieux Carré (p50), founded in 1916 and still going strong

V

GAY & LESBIAN NEW ORLEANS

New Orleans has always been a haven for the outsiders and eccentrics of the American South, and while gays and lesbians are not necessarily any of the above, they've certainly been pejoratively viewed as such in the past. Men and women of a 'particular persuasion' historically flocked here, where their relationships were studiously ignored, if not outright accepted.

Today New Orleans has one of the most vibrant gay and lesbian scenes in America, a self-confidence built on the foundations of the above history. Festivals like **Southern Decadence** (www.southerndecadence.net) and **Gay Pride New Orleans** (www.gayprideneworleans.com) are embraced by the entire city, a scene that may surprise those used to the generally conservative South.

There are a few facets to the local LGBT scene, but these sub-communities converge on Faubourg Marigny and the Fauborg Marigny Book Store (p56), the oldest gay bookstore in the South. From here your options diverge based on geographic orientation. Head north further into Faubourg Marigny for cozy sports bars and Country Western honky tonks that serve an older if still fun-loving crowd of bears, bikers etc. South of here you enter the French Quarter and its loud, thumping scene. This territory is fun, if predictable: muscle shirts, tight pants and lots of waxed bodies.

That said, the straight and gay scenes here tend to blend very seamlessly, perhaps partly because of a love for live music (the backbone of local nightlife) that transcends sexuality. The **Country Club New Orleans** (www .thecountryclubneworleans.com) runs events. Check out the websites www.gay neworleans.com and www.neworleansgaytravel.com for listings and event information.

Not-so-lonesome cowboys celebrate Mardi Gras (p10) in the French Quarter

FILM

New Orleans is one of the most photogenic cities in America, so it shouldn't come as much surprise she's one of the most filmed spots in the country as well. This city has one of the most unique senses of place in the country – you can't look down the street here and *not* know you're in New Orleans – and a lot of filmmakers have tried to capture this special quality in their work. It helps that the city offers very lucrative tax credits to folks who want to make movies here; for information on that program and movies being filmed in the city during your visit, check out www .filmneworleans.org.

We've provided the following list of New Orleans films and filming locations, but we also want to call attention to documentaries that give a good peek beneath the city's surface. *Trouble the Water* (2008) and *When the Levees Broke* (2006) are two of the best films on the impact and after-effects of Hurricane Katrina, while *Tootie's Last Suit* (2006) delves into both the culture of Mardi Gras Indians and a particularly fascinating family drama between a 'Big Chief' of an Indian tribe and his successor.

CLASSIC CINEMATIC NEW ORLEANS
> *King Creole* (1958) Opens on Bourbon St (p38).
> *Angel Heart* (1987) Has a scene in the Maple Leaf (p99).
> *Pretty Baby* (1978) Brooke Shields as a streetwalker in the Columns (p97).
> *A Streetcar Named Desire* (1951)
> *Easy Rider* (1969) Dennis Hopper and Peter Fonda smoke pot in St Louis Cemetery (p107).

NEW NOLA IN THE MOVIES
> *Interview with the Vampire* (1994) Scenes shot on the city waterfront.
> *The Pelican Brief* (1993) Partly filmed in Tulane University (p90).
> *All the King's Men* (2006) Filmed all over the city.
> *Tremé* (2009) HBO series filmed in its namesake neighborhood (p100).
> *The Curious Case of Benjamin Button* (2008) Watch for the Clover Grill (p46).

ONLY IN NEW ORLEANS

In a way, every moment here is an 'only in New Orleans' moment.

Well, c'mon. What other American cities have Indian tribes composed entirely of African Americans who decided to out-'pretty' their rivals and show off their respective 'shine' via huge feathered costumes? What town essentially defines itself via an annual festival (Mardi Gras) that begins with men in skeleton suits and signs proclaiming 'You Next' marching out of a cemetery followed by old ladies dressed either as prostitutes or dolls or both (historical records disagree). Who are *then* followed by African Americans in *black face* tossing coconuts and an entire *white* parade that celebrates the overturning of authority by venerating a hyperbolic court of royalty called 'Rex?' Check out the Backstreet Cultural Museum (p101) or the Presbytère (p43) for more Mardi Gras details.

Where else do US Military brass instruments get turned into the component parts of a genre of dance music that could get the stiffest corpse jigging out of Le Bon Temps Roulé (p98)? Where else is a dude in a homemade breast plate with a pair of spoons considered a musical genius and an integral part of a zydeco band?

'Only in New Orleans, baby' is the motto of a lot of citizens of this city. Because 'only in New Orleans' is where they choose to be.

Voodoo altar – New Orleans is the US city most closely associated with voodoo (p147)

>BACKGROUND

Up close and personal with a Mississippi riverboat (p50)

BACKGROUND
HISTORY
NATIVE INHABITANTS

Louisiana was well-settled and cultivated by the time of European arrival. Spanish explorers reported sighting hundreds of villages in southern Louisiana as early as the 16th century. Contrary to the myth of hunter-gatherers living in a state of harmony with the forest, local Native Americans significantly altered and had an impact on their environment with roads, trade networks and infrastructure. Ironically, by the time the French arrived with the goal of colonization, the region had probably reverted to something like a state of nature due to the massive deaths caused by introduced diseases.

After 1700, Europeans documented numerous direct contacts with local tribes. A confederation known collectively as the Muskogeans lived north of Lake Pontchartrain and occasionally settled along the banks of the Mississippi River. The Houma nation thrived in isolated coastal bayous from Terrebonne to Lafourche up until the 1940s. Alliances between escaped African slaves and Native Americans were not uncommon, and are considered the foundation of the modern African American Mardi Gras Indian phenomenon.

THE FRENCH & SPANISH ARRIVE

The Mississippi eluded in-depth European exploration until 1699, when Canadian-born Pierre Le Moyne d'Iberville, Sieur d'Iberville, and his younger brother Jean-Baptiste Le Moyne de Bienville, Sieur de Bienville, located the muddy outflow. They encamped 40 miles downriver from present-day New Orleans on the eve of Mardi Gras and, knowing their countrymen would be celebrating the pre-Lenten holiday, christened the small spit of land Pointe de Mardi Gras – fitting.

Iberville died of yellow fever in 1706, but Bienville remained in Louisiana to found Nouvelle Orléans (so named in honor of the duc d'Orléans) in 1718. Bienville chose a small patch of relatively high ground beside Bayou St John, which connected the Mississippi to Lake Pontchartrain and offered more direct access to the Gulf of Mexico. Factoring in the site's strategic position, Bienville's party decided to overlook the hazards of perennial flooding and mosquito-borne diseases. Engineer Adrien de Pauger's severe grid plan, drawn in 1722, still delineates the French Quarter today.

Bienville's original group of 30 ex-convicts, six carpenters and four Canadians struggled against floods and yellow-fever epidemics. The colony, in the meantime, was promoted as heaven on earth to unsuspecting French, Germans and Swiss, who soon began arriving in New Orleans by the shipload. To augment these numbers, additional convicts and prostitutes were freed from French jails if they agreed to relocate to Louisiana. To increase the female population, the Ursuline nuns brought young, marriageable girls with them in 1728. Looking about her, one recently arrived nun commented that 'the devil here has a very large empire,' proving that even in those early days New Orleans had a reputation for the ribald.

In 1762 France handed the unprofitable Louisiana Territory to King Charles III of Spain in return for an ally against England. But the 'Frenchness' of New Orleans was little affected for the duration of Spain's control. The main enduring impact left by the Spanish was the architecture of the Quarter. After fires decimated the French Quarter in 1788 and 1794, much of it was rebuilt by the Spanish; consequently, the quaint French Quarter we know today is predominantly Spanish in style.

The Spanish sensed they might eventually have to fight the expansion-minded Americans to retain control of the lower Mississippi. Hence, Spain jumped at Napoleon Bonaparte's offer to retake control of Louisiana in 1800.

ANTEBELLUM PROSPERITY

Napoleon needed cash to finance his wars, and US President Thomas Jefferson coveted control of the Mississippi. Nevertheless, Robert Livingston, the US minister in Paris, was astonished by Bonaparte's offer to sell the entire Louisiana Territory – an act that would double the US's size – for $15 million. On December 20, 1803, the American flag was raised.

Little cheer arose from the Creole community, who figured the Americans' Protestant beliefs, support for English common law and puritan work ethic jarred with the Catholic Creole way of life. In 1808 the territorial legislature adopted elements of Spanish and French law in order to preserve Creole culture, a legacy that uniquely persists in Louisiana today, to the frustration of many a Tulane law student.

New Orleans grew quickly under US control, becoming the fourth-wealthiest city in the world and second-largest port in the US in a matter of years. The city's population grew as well, and spilled beyond the borders of the French Quarter. In the 1830s Samuel Jarvis Peters bought plantation land upriver from the French Quarter to build a distinctly American section – today, the beginning of the CBD at Canal St. Developers further transformed 15 riverbank plantations into the lush American suburbs of Lafayette, Jefferson and Carrollton, currently all part of Uptown.

Obviously, the wealthy chose the highest ground for their enclaves, while the city drained low-lying wetlands for settlement by immigrants and blacks. These neighborhoods remain prone to flooding.

On a much lighter note, the late 1850s saw the revival of Carnival. The old Creole tradition, now propelled by Americans, hit the streets as a much grander affair than ever before – the first taste of modern Mardi Gras.

MULTICULTI GUMBO

The French brought some 1300 African slaves to New Orleans in the city's first decade. In 1724, French Louisianans adopted the Code Noir (Black Code), a document that carefully restricted the social position of blacks, but also addressed some of the needs of slaves and accorded certain privileges to free persons of color.

Long before the start of the Civil War, New Orleans had the South's largest population of free blacks, known in Creole New Orleans as *les gens de couleur libre* (free people of color). Considered a highly cultured class, free blacks probably enjoyed a higher quality of life than blacks

CLOSING THE CONGO SQUARE CIRCLE

Near the main entrance to Louis Armstrong Park (p106) is one of the most important spots, arguably, in the development of modern music: Congo Sq. Originally known as 'Place de Negres,' this area was once just outside the city's walls (Rampart St, as the name suggests, was the town limit). Under the Code Noir (Black Code), slaves were allowed to gather here on Sundays on their days off. The period of rest became one of both celebration and preservation of West African ritual, which largely revolved around song and dance. Sundays became a way of letting off steam and channeling latent discontent, and it must have been, at the time, the largest celebration of traditional African culture in continental North America – slaves were forbidden from such practices in the American colonies.

The tradition was shut down when American settlers took over New Orleans, but it was alive long enough to imprint its musical traces into the city's cultural substrate. By the late 19th century, brass bands were blending these African rhythms with classical music imported by European settlers and French-educated old New Orleanians. The bands played on a weekly basis in Congo Sq, and their sound eventually evolved, especially near the bordellos of nearby Storyville, into jazz – itself the foundation for the variations of pop music (rhythm and blues, rock and roll, even hip-hop) America would give the world in the 20th century.

(and even many whites) anywhere else in the US. They were often well educated, and some owned land and slaves. But they didn't share all the rights and privileges of white Creoles and Americans, barred as they were from voting or serving in juries.

Affairs between races were socially accepted, but interracial marriage was not. The *plaçage* was a cultural institution whereby white Creole men 'kept' light-skinned black women, providing them with a handsome wardrobe and a cottage in the Vieux Carré, and supporting any resulting children. Subtle gradations of mixed color led to a complex class structure in which those with the least African blood tended to enjoy the greatest privileges (octoroons, for instance, who were in theory one-eighth black, rated higher than quadroons, who were one-quarter black).

The multicultural stew wasn't limited to people of African descent, and the European influence expanded beyond the French. German immigrants frequently Gallicized their names and blended into the soup. Former French subjects arrived from St Domingue (now Haiti), bringing voodoo. Irish and Jewish immigrants came in the 19th century, to the point that antebellum New Orleans was the second-largest gateway, after New York, for immigrants entering the US.

At the dawn of the Civil War, New Orleans was by far the most prosperous city south of the Mason-Dixon Line. On January 26, 1861, Louisiana became the sixth state to secede from the Union, and on March 21 the state joined the Confederacy – but not for very long. The Union captured New Orleans in April 1862 and held it till the end of the war.

New Orleanians, otherwise famous for their hospitality, didn't take too kindly to the occupation government or its leader, Major General Benjamin 'Beast' Butler. As his nickname suggests, Butler was not intent on winning the hearts and minds. Soon after the US flag went up in front of the US Mint, a local man named William Mumford cut it down. Butler hung Mumford from the very same flagpole. Toilet bowls were soon being imprinted with Butler's visage.

INTO THE MODERN AGE

At the war's end Louisiana's state constitution was redrawn. Causing no small amount of resentment among white Southerners, full suffrage was granted to blacks, but the same rights were denied to former Confederate soldiers and rebel sympathizers. Emboldened, blacks began challenging discrimination laws, but many of the civil liberties that blacks were supposed to have gained after the Civil War were reversed by what became known as Jim Crow laws, which reinforced and in some ways increased segregation and inequality between blacks and whites. In 1896 Homer Plessy, whose one-eighth African lineage subjected him to segregation statutes, challenged the law in the landmark *Plessy v. Ferguson* case. Although Plessy's case exposed the arbitrary nature of Jim Crow laws, the US Supreme Court interpreted the Constitution as providing political, not social, equality and ruled to uphold 'separate but equal' statutes. 'Separate but equal' remained the law of the land until the Plessy case was overturned by *Brown v. the Board of Education* in 1954. Congress passed the Civil Rights Act in 1964, which reversed the remainder of Jim Crow legislation.

The 20th century dawned with the emergence of a new musical style called 'jass' – and later jazz – a combination of black Creole musicianship and African American rhythms, which became a fundamental contribution to city culture. Tourists, attracted by the city's music and food (and infamous nightlife), became more of a focal point of the New Orleans economy; as a result, the city began to preserve its historic neighborhoods.

In the 1930s, oil companies began dredging canals and laying a massive pipe infrastructure (for pumping oil from the Gulf of Mexico) throughout the bayou region to the southwest of New Orleans. This new industry contributed to the erosion of Louisiana's coastal wetlands, but it also became another driving engine of the state economy.

The demographics of the city dramatically shifted during the 'white flight' years, chiefly the period after WWII and, later, desegregation. Black residents settled in the inner city, while whites relocated to suburbs like Metairie. Freeways were built and high-rise office buildings and hotels shot up around the CBD. In 1978 New Orleans elected its first black mayor, Ernest 'Dutch' Morial, whose term ended in 1986. In 1994 his son Marc Morial was elected mayor. The younger Morial attempted to pass a referendum in 2001 permitting him to run for a third term, but the city electorate turned him down in favor of another African American, businessman Ray Nagin in 2002. The city was due to elect a new mayor in 2010.

In 2005 Hurricane Katrina struck and the city's levee system failed. The city was evacuated and experienced, according to the US Census Bureau, an almost 54% drop in population. As residents streamed back, the population rose by 13.8% from 2006–7, the fastest growth of any large American city. The 2010 US Census had not been completed at the time of research, but in 2009 the *Times-Picayune* estimated the city's population to be 469,605 households, about 88.1% of pre-Katrina levels for the metro area; 74% in the city of New Orleans itself.

LIFE AS A NEW ORLEANIAN

Describing what it means to be a New Orleanian depends, of course, on what kind of New Orleanian you are. To generalize, there is an upper, middle and lower class in this city, and these lines are largely drawn by color and geography. Interrupting this balance is the displacement of thousands of largely African American residents and the arrival of thousands of rebuilding professionals and Latinos.

This is still a majority black (60%) town; the rest of the population is mainly white, largely descended from a milieu of French, Anglo, German, Irish and Italian settlers. The 3% of the population that identifies as Asian is mostly Vietnamese and lives in outlying neighborhoods like Gretna, Versailles and New Orleans East; having arrived following the Vietnam War and successfully establishing themselves in society, their story is that of the American Dream. The Latino population is officially around 4.5%, but this is probably an underestimate given illegal immigration. Many local Latinos, especially new arrivals, are from Honduras, and are employed in construction and other manual labor fields. A sure sign of Latino establishment: in 2009, a Mardi Gras krewe was formed for new arrivals from 'south of the border.'

Roughly, there is a 36% chance you're Catholic in New Orleans (the city, incidentally, has one of the largest African American Catholic populations in the country) and even if you're not, you're probably familiar with the rhythms of Catholic ritual – Mardi Gras, after all, has its roots in the Church calendar. If you're not Catholic, you're probably Christian of some denomination, although there are between 7000 to 10,000 Jews here, one of the larger (and older) concentrations in the South. Or you could have no religion at all, estimated to be the fastest growing belief system in America according to the Pew Forum on Religion & Public Life. Despite the city's boosterism of voodoo, there are few actual practitioners of that religion, although some Latinos may practice a version of voodoo from the Caribbean called Santeria.

Statistics in certain areas are difficult to measure post-Katrina, but as of 2007 the median household income in New Orleans was around $38,600, while the national median household income was roughly $50,200. But New Orleanians have traditionally had a lower cost of living compared to the rest of the country. That said, home insurance rates have always been (and since the storm have become even more so) prohibitively high. Rents also have increased, especially in those parts of the city that occupy high

RELIEF ORGANIZATIONS

If you've stuck to the neighborhoods we've described in this book, you may leave New Orleans thinking the city has entirely recovered from Hurricane Katrina. It hasn't. There are still huge swathes of town that remain devastated, and the population in the city itself hovers around 74% of pre-hurricane levels. The rebuilding process is ongoing; here are some organizations you may want to consider contacting if you'd like to lend a hand.

Bush-Clinton Katrina Fund (www.bushclintonkatrinafund.org) Founded by the former presidents; funds numerous Gulf Coast rebuilding and restoration projects.

Common Ground Relief (☎ 304-9097; www.commongroundrelief.org; 1800 Deslonde St) Community rebuilding volunteer organization that provides a free legal clinic, job training and works on wetland reclamation projects.

Gulf Restoration Network (Map pp64-5, D3; ☎ 525-1528; http://healthygulf.org; 338 Baronne St) Works to preserve and restore the wetlands and coastal environment that is integral, among other things, to flood protection on the Gulf Coast.

Make It Right (www.makeitrightnola.org) Brad Pitt's pet project aims to build affordable, environmentally friendly housing in wrecked portions of the Lower Ninth Ward.

New Orleans Area Habitat for Humanity (Map pp88-9, C3; ☎ 861-4121; www.habitat-nola.org; 7100 St Charles Ave) One of the prime movers for home reconstruction in the city.

Parkway Partners (Map pp64-5, D5; ☎ 620-2224; www.parkwayparntersnola.org; 1137 Baronne St) Plants community gardens and works to build up public green spaces.

Project Home Again (www.projecthomeagain.net; PO Box 851008, New Orleans, LA 70185) Run by Barnes & Noble founder Leonard Riggio. Works to repopulate Gentilly, one of the city's most historically mixed middle-class neighborhoods, by building new homes exclusively for Gentilly homeowners who lost their houses; these homeowners can trade in their old deeds for a Project Home Again building.

Two good information clearinghouses on relief efforts are www.hurricanekatrinarelief.com and www.katrinarelief.org. Check out www.nola.com/katrina/graphics/flashflood.swf for an excellent graphic on the evolution of the flood in the city.

ground and were unaffected by the floodwaters. And it costs a lot – sometimes tens of thousands of dollars – to remodel homes to meet flood protection standards. On the bright side, homeowner initiatives are increasing, and buying a home in one of the city's many heritage districts qualifies one for pretty generous tax breaks.

Access to certain commodities remains problematic. Many large grocery stores were closed and remained so after the storm. A 2009 Tulane University study demonstrated that low-income residents often have to travel long distances to procure healthy foods and, in lieu of those options, often fall back on cheap snack-food options available at corner stores.

In general, New Orleanians who can afford it drive, send their children to private school and eat out quite a bit. Those who can't afford it, rely on the city for public transportation, education etc. Increasingly, nonprofit organizations and grassroots community groups are taking on the role of providing or augmenting many city services. It's the new New Orleans way. In April 2009, political strategist James Carville determined New Orleanians have more civic pride than citizens of any other comparably sized American city. For all the hardship we've described, this is still New Orleans. There's no other place like it. And folks here, from old-line residents to recent arrivals, aren't giving up on home.

DIRECTORY
TRANSPORTATION
ARRIVAL & DEPARTURE
AIR

Louis Armstrong New Orleans International Airport (MSY; ☎ 464-0831; www.flymsy.com) is in the suburb of Kenner, 11 miles west of the city along the I-10 freeway. It's a small airport with only one terminal, so it's pretty easy to get around. Shuttles, buses and cabs depart regularly from the curb, outside the baggage claim area.

TO/FROM THE AIRPORT
Bus

If your baggage is not too unwieldy and you're in no hurry, **Jefferson Transit** (☎ 818-1077; www.jeffersontransit.org) offers the cheapest ride downtown aboard its Airport Downtown Express for $1.60. At the airport the bus stops along the median on the second level, near the Delta counter. The ride to New Orleans follows city streets, pausing for stoplights every few minutes, and will only get you as far as the corner of Tulane St and Carrollton Ave. From here it's a cheap cab ride to the French Quarter, or you can transfer to an **RTA** (☎ 248-3900; www.norta.com) bus. Bus 27 will get you to St Charles Ave in the Garden District; bus 39 follows Tulane Ave to Canal St, just outside the French Quarter.

Car

The quickest way to drive between the airport and downtown is to take I-10 freeway. If you're coming from downtown on I-10, take exit 223 for the airport; going to downtown, take exit 234, as the Superdome looms before you. Traffic can get very slow near the Huey Long Bridge. If traffic is light, it's a 20-minute drive to most of town; if the roads are clogged, it can take 40 minutes or more

CLIMATE CHANGE & TRAVEL

Travel – especially air travel – is a significant contributor to global climate change. At Lonely Planet, we believe that all travelers have a responsibility to limit their personal impact. As a result, we have teamed with Rough Guides and other concerned industry partners to support Climate Care, which allows travelers to offset the greenhouse gases they are responsible for with contributions to energy-saving projects and other climate-friendly initiatives in the developing world. Lonely Planet offsets all staff and author travel. For more information, turn to the responsible-travel pages on www.lonelyplanet.com. For details on offsetting your carbon emissions and a carbon calculator, go to www.climatecare.org.

OTHER THAN THE AIRPORT...

Look, Steve Goodman wrote a damn song about a train called 'The City of New Orleans.' You don't have to fly here. Consider giving some relief to your wallet and the Earth by opting for one of the options listed here...

Greyhound (☎ 800-231-2222; www.greyhound.com) buses arrive and depart at New Orleans **Union Passenger Terminal** (☎ 528-1610; 1001 Loyola Ave), which is also known as Union Station. It's seven blocks upriver from Canal St. Greyhound regularly connects to Lafayette, Opelousas and Baton Rouge, LA; Clarksdale, MS; and Memphis, TN, en route to essentially every city in the USA.

Three **Amtrak** (☎ 800-872-7245) trains serve New Orleans at the Union Passenger Terminal. The *City of New Orleans* train runs to Memphis, TN; Jackson, MS; and Chicago, IL. Alternatively, the *Crescent Route* serves Birmingham, AL; Atlanta, GA; Washington, DC; and New York City, NY. The *Sunset Limited* route between Los Angeles, CA and Miami, FL, also passes through New Orleans.

Shuttle

Most visitors take the **Airport Shuttle** (☎ 522-3500; www.airportshuttlenew orleans.com) to and from the airport. It's a frequent service between the airport and downtown hotels for $15 per passenger each way. It's a cheap introduction to the city, although it can be time-consuming, especially if your hotel is the last stop. At the airport, buy tickets from agencies in the baggage claim area. For your return to the airport, call a day ahead to arrange for a pick-up, which you should schedule at least two hours prior to your check-in time.

Taxi

A taxi ride from the airport costs a flat rate of $28 for one to two passengers. Each additional passenger costs another $12. No more than four passengers are allowed in a single cab.

VISAS

A passport with an official visa is required for most visitors to the USA; contact the American embassy or consulate in your home country for more information. Visitors between the ages of 14 and 79 have to be interviewed before a visa is granted, and all applicants must pay fees that currently stand at $131. You'll also have to prove you're not trying to stay in the USA permanently. If you are traveling for 90 days or less you may qualify for the Visa Waiver Program (VWP); currently citizens of 43 countries are eligible for the above. Learn more at http://travel.state.gov/ visa/temp/without/without_1990. html. The Electronic System for

Transportation Time Between Key Destinations

	French Quarter	Central Business District (CBD)	Faubourg Marigny
French Quarter		walk 10min; taxi 5–10min	walk 10min; taxi 5–10min
Central Business District (CBD)	walk 10min; taxi 5–10min		walk 20–30min; taxi 10min; bus 10–20min
Faubourg Marigny	walk 10min; taxi 5–10min	walk 20–30min; taxi 10min	bus 10–20min
Magazine St (Lower Garden District)	walk (to CBD) & streetcar around 30min; taxi 15–20min	walk 30–45min; taxi 10–15min; bus 10–25min; streetcar 10–20min	taxi 20–30min; bus 40 or more minutes
City Park	walk (to CBD) & streetcar 25–45min; taxi 15min	streetcar 20–30min; taxi 15min; bus 30min	bus 30 or more minutes; taxi 20min

Travel Authorization determines if you are eligible for the VWP; its website can be found at https://esta.cbp.dhs.gov. For general visa information, see http://travel.state.gov/visa/temp/types/types_1262.html£6.

GETTING AROUND

Getting around New Orleans isn't too difficult, although public transportation is pretty wanting. You can walk between neighborhoods featured in this book if they're adjacent to each other, and it's certainly possible to walk from the French Quarter to the Garden District, but it is a hike, and in the hot summer months you're asking for a sweat bath. Keep in mind neighborhoods here go from wealthy to poor to potentially dangerous within the space of a block. If you're walking around

Magazine St, be careful of straying too far south toward the river; ditto walking north of St Claude Ave if you're in Faubourg Marigny and the Bywater.

BICYCLE

New Orleans is flat and relatively compact, but watch out for heavy traffic, potholes and bad neighborhoods. All state-operated ferries offer free transportation for bikes. Bicyclists board ahead of cars by walking down the left lane of the ramp to the swinging gate. You must wait for the cars to exit before leaving. The Regional Transit Authority (RTA) doesn't allow bikes on streetcars or buses unless you have a two-parish permit, which is inconvenient for casual visitors. Bikes can be rented for around $25 a day at **Bicycle Michael's** (Map p53, A3; ☎ 945-9505; http://bicyclemichaels.com; 622

Magazine St (Lower Garden District)	City Park
walk (to CBD) & streetcar around 30min; taxi 15-20min	walk (to CBD) & streetcar 25-45min; taxi 15min
walk 30-45min; taxi 10-15min; bus 10-25min; streetcar 10-20min	streetcar 20-30min; bus 30min; taxi 15min
bus 40 or more minutes; taxi 20-30min	bus 30 or more minutes; taxi 20min
	bus 30 or more minutes; streetcar & walk 40min-1 hr; taxi 20-30min
bus 30 or more minutes; streetcar & walk 40min-1hr; taxi 20-30min	

Frenchmen St) in Faubourg Marigny or for $30 a day from **Mike the Bike Guy** (Map pp88-9, F5; ☎ 899-1344; 4411 Magazine St) in Uptown.

BUS

The **Regional Transit Authority** (RTA; ☎ 827-7433; www.norta.com) offers bus and streetcar services. Fares are $1.25, plus 25¢ for a transfer. Service is decent, but you wouldn't want to solely rely on public transport during a New Orleans visit. No buses run through the heart of the French Quarter, so most visitors only use them when venturing Uptown or out to City Park.

CAR

A car is a good thing to have in New Orleans, but if you're planning to spend most of your time in the French Quarter or CBD, don't bother. You'll just end up wasting money on parking.

Here are the main things to watch out for when driving in New Orleans. First: potholes. The city streets are in an atrocious state, and tires here, accordingly, have short life spans. Tricky left turns through the very common four-way intersections, and the intersections themselves, can be a hazard. While stop signs are set out in residential areas, not everyone obeys them. New Orleanian friendliness can be annoying if people stop their cars in the middle of a narrow street to chat with someone – every New Orleans driver has a story about this. Finally, New Orleans drivers are terrible turn signalers. Try to keep your head from exploding the fifth time you get cut off.

Visitors from abroad may find it wise to back up their national driver's license with an International

WHERE ARE YOU AT?

The Mississippi River serves as a false compass in New Orleans. While it's true that the river flows from north to south, it curves below New Orleans and, thus, is actually flowing from west to east where it passes the French Quarter. When locals give directions, they rarely indicate north, south, east or west. Directions, upriver or downriver, are relative to the water flow — for example, 'the Convention Center is upriver (ie above) from the French Quarter', even though a compass would show that the Convention Center is south-southwest (ie below).

In addition, the river and Lake Pontchartrain serve as landmarks in 'riverside' or 'lakeside' directions: 'you'll find Louis Armstrong Park on the lakeside of the French Quarter' and 'Preservation Hall is on St Peter St toward the river from Bourbon St.'

Driving Permit, available from their local automobile club.

Parking

Downtown on-street parking is typically for short-term use. In some parts of town, look for the solar-powered parking meters. One meter often serves an entire block, so if there's no meter on the curb immediately beside your car, don't assume it means parking is free. And of course there are all kinds of restrictions for street cleaning that limit when you can park on certain streets. There are all sorts of pay lots in the French Quarter and CBD.

Vehicles parked illegally are frequently towed in the Quarter. If you park your car in a driveway, within 20ft of a corner or crosswalk, within 15ft of a fire hydrant or on a street-sweeping day, you will need to pay about $75 to $100 (cash or credit card) plus cab fare to retrieve your car

from the **Auto Pound** (Map pp102-3, G5; ☎ 565-7450; 400 N Claiborne Ave).

Outside of the Quarter and downtown, parking is a cinch. There's plenty of street parking and not many restrictions. With that said, be careful of street parking during Mardi Gras and Jazz Fest, when cops are liable to ticket you for any loophole of an infraction.

Rental

Most of the big car-rental companies are found in New Orleans, particularly at the airport. Typically you must be at least 25 years of age and have a major credit card, as well as a valid driver's license, in order to rent a car.

Rates go up and availability lessens during special events or large conventions. A compact car typically costs $30 to $40 a day or $150 to $200 a week. On top of that, there is a 13.75% tax and an optional $9 to $15 a day loss/damage-waiver or LDW (insurance).

If you already have auto insurance you're probably covered, but check with your insurance company first.

Agencies in or near the downtown area include:

Avis (off Map pp64-5, B1; ☎ 523-4317, 800-3311-1212; 2024 Canal St)

Budget Rent-a-Car (Map pp64-5, D1; ☎ 565-5600; 1317 Canal St)

Hertz (Map pp64-5, F6; ☎ 568-1645; 901 Convention Center Blvd)

FERRY

The Canal St ferry (Map pp40–1) operates between Canal St and the West Bank community of Algiers from 6am to midnight daily. Another ferry stops at Jackson Ave, near the Irish Channel, and leads to the suburb of Gretna. The ferries are free for pedestrians and cyclists, and just $1 for vehicles.

STREETCAR

Fare is from $1.25 to $1.50.

Canal Streetcar Lines

Bright red streetcars began running up and down Canal St in 2004. They look old, but aren't. All are modern, air-conditioned light-rail cars custom designed and built locally.

Two slightly different lines follow Canal St to Mid-City. Both run from the French Market and up the levee before heading up Canal St. The 47 line goes all the way to City Park

Ave. More useful for tourists is the 8 line, which heads up a spur on N Carrollton Ave, ending up at the Esplanade Ave entrance to City Park. The cars run from 6am to 11pm.

Riverfront Streetcar Line

In 1988 the wheelchair-accessible Riverfront streetcar line began operating vintage red cars on the old dockside rail corridor wedged between the levee and flood wall. The 2-mile route runs between the French Market, in the lower end of the French Quarter near Esplanade Ave, and the upriver Convention Center, crossing Canal St on the way. It operates from 6am to midnight.

St Charles Ave Streetcar Line

When the St Charles Ave streetcar route opened as the New Orleans & Carrollton Railroad in 1835, it was the nation's second horse-drawn streetcar line. The line was also among the first systems to be electrified when New Orleans adopted electric traction in 1893. Now it runs from Canal St to the intersection of Claiborne and Carrollton Aves.

TAXI

If you are traveling alone or at night, taxis are highly recommended. **United Cab** (☎ 522-9771) is the biggest and most reliable company in New Orleans. You might have to call for a pick-up, unless you are in a central part of the French Quarter, where it is relatively easy to flag down a passing cab.

Fares within the city start with a $2.50 flag fall charge for one passenger (plus $1 for each additional passenger and a $2 fuel surcharge). From there it's $1.60 per mile. Practically speaking, this amounts to fares of around $11 from the French Quarter to the Bywater and $13 or more to the Garden District. Don't forget to tip your driver 10% to 15%.

PRACTICALITIES

BUSINESS HOURS

Shops and stores are usually open from 10am to 7pm on weekdays, and till 2pm on weekends. Banks are open 9am to 5pm on weekdays, and from 8am to noon on Saturday. Restaurants are usually open from 11am to 11pm, and are closed either Sunday or Monday (or both). Bars tend to open around 5pm, and while 2am is generally a reliable last call on weekdays, they really don't shut till the last customer leaves (or gets thrown out).

EMBASSIES

Canada's nearest consulate is in Miami, FL.
France (☎ 523-5772; www.consulfrance -nouvelleorleans.org; 1340 Poydras St)

UK Honorary Consul (☎ 524-4180; 10th fl, 321 St Charles Ave)

EMERGENCIES

Ambulance, fire & police ☎ 911
Police (nonemergency) ☎ 821-2222

HOLIDAYS

Note that when national holidays fall on a weekend, they are often celebrated on the nearest Friday or Monday so that everyone enjoys a three-day weekend. For further information on New Orleans' holidays and festivals, see p23. The following are all national holidays.
New Year's Day January 1
Presidents' Day Third Monday in February
Memorial Day Last Monday in May
Independence Day July 4
Labor Day First Monday in September
Columbus Day Second Monday in October
Veterans Day November 11
Thanksgiving Fourth Thursday in November

INTERNET ACCESS

Many hotels offer internet access, but it's not yet something you can assume – be sure to confirm while making reservations. Wi-fi hot spots (free access for those carrying laptops with wireless capability) are becoming increasingly common in cafes – any of the numerous Community Coffee, Starbucks and PJs coffee houses found throughout town offer this service.

New Orleans Public Library (Map pp64-5, D2; ☎ 529-7323; http://nutrias. org; 219 Loyola Ave), near City Hall, has terminals for free web access.

INTERNET RESOURCES

There's no better place to start your web explorations than the Lonely Planet website at www .lonelyplanet.com. Here you'll find succinct summaries on traveling to most places on earth, postcards from other travelers and the Thorn Tree bulletin board, where you can ask questions before you go or dispense advice when you get back.

Other useful websites, many of which serve as gateways to an infinite number of interesting links:
Gambit Weekly (www.bestofneworleans.com)
Jazz Festival (www.nojazzfest.com)
Louisiana Music Factory (www.louisiana musicfactory.com)
Nola Fun Guide (www.nolafunguide.com)
Offbeat Magazine (www.offbeat.com)
Times-Picayune (www.nola.com)
WWOZ Radio (www.wwoz.org)

MEDICAL SERVICES

If you need immediate medical attention and you are in your hotel, your first call should be to the front desk. Some of the larger hotels have agreements with on-call doctors who can make house calls if necessary. In really urgent situations, you can call an **ambulance** (☎ 911), which will deliver you to a hospital emergency room. If you

can get to an emergency room with the help of a friend, your best bet is the **Tulane University Medical Center** (Map pp64-5, C2; ☎ 988-5800; 1415 Tulane Ave), located in the CBD, and **Touro Infirmary** (Map pp76-7, A6; ☎ 897-7011; 1401 Foucher St), in the Lower Garden District.

POST

New Orleans' **main post office** (Map pp64-5, C4; ☎ 589-1135; 701 Loyola Ave) is near City Hall. There are smaller branches throughout the city, including the **Airport Mail Center** (☎ 589-1296) in the passenger terminal; the **World Trade Center** (Map pp64-5, G3; ☎ 524-0033; 2 Canal St); and in the CBD at **Lafayette Sq** (Map pp64-5, E4; ☎ 524-0491; 610 S Maestri Pl). Post offices are generally open 8:30am to 4:30pm Monday to Friday and 8:30am to noon Saturday. Postal rates frequently increase, but at the time of writing the rates were 44¢ for first-class mail within the USA and 24¢ for postcards.

It costs 75¢ to send a 1oz letter to Canada, 79¢ to Mexico and 98¢ to other countries.

The **US Postal Service** (☎ 800-222-1811; www.usps.gov) also offers a Priority Mail service, which delivers your letter or package anywhere in the USA in two days or less. The cost is $4.95 for 1lb. For heavier items, rates differ according to the distance mailed. Overnight Express Mail starts at $15.

SAFETY

Exercise the caution you would in any US city. The possibility of getting mugged is something to consider even in areas you'd think are safe (eg the Garden District). Naturally, solo pedestrians are targeted more often than people walking in groups, and daytime is a better time to be out on foot than nighttime. That said, don't be paranoid – just don't be naive either.

Pedestrians crossing the street do not have the right of way and motorists (unless they are from out of state) will not yield. Whether on foot or in a car, be wary before entering an intersection, as New Orleans drivers are notorious for running yellow, and even red, lights.

TAXES & REFUNDS

New Orleans' 9% sales tax is tacked onto virtually everything, including meals, groceries and car rentals. For accommodations, room and occupancy taxes add an additional 12% to your bill plus $1 to $3 per person, depending on the size of the hotel.

Some merchants in Louisiana participate in a program called **Louisiana Tax Free Shopping** (☎ 568-5323; www.louisianataxfree.com). Look for the snazzy red-and-blue 'tax free' logo in the window or on the sign of the store. Usually these stores specialize in the kinds of impulse purchases people are likely to make while on vacation. In these stores, present a passport to verify you are not a US citizen and request a voucher as you make your purchase. Reimbursement centers are located in the **Downtown Refund Center** (☎ 568-3605; Riverwalk Mall; ☼ 10am-3:30pm) and the main lobby of the **Louis Armstrong Airport** (☎ 467-0723; ☼ 8:30am-4:30pm Mon-Fri, 9am-1pm Sat & Sun).

TELEPHONE

The New Orleans area code is ☎ 504, which includes Thibodaux and the surrounding area. Baton Rouge and its surrounding area use the area code ☎ 225. Area code ☎ 318 applies to the northern part of the state.

TIME

New Orleans Standard Time is six hours behind GMT/UTC. That puts it one hour behind the east coast of the USA, and two hours ahead of the west coast. In early April the clocks move ahead one hour for daylight saving time; clocks move back one hour in October.

TIPPING

Tipping is not optional. In bars and restaurants the waitstaff are paid minimal wages and rely on tips for their livelihood. The service has to be absolutely appalling before you consider not tipping. Tip at least 15% of the bill or 20% if the service is good. New Orleanians who have either worked in or been connected to the service industry are often heavy tippers. You needn't tip at fast-food restaurants or self-serve cafeterias.

Taxi drivers expect a 15% tip. If you stay at a top-end hotel, tipping is so common you might get tennis elbow from reaching for your wallet constantly. Hotel porters who carry bags a long way expect $3 to $5, or $1 per bag; smaller services (holding the taxi door open for you) might justify only $1. Valet parking is worth about $2, and is given when your car is returned to you.

TOILETS
A recording by Benny Grunch, 'Ain't No Place to Pee on Mardi Gras Day,' summarizes the situation in the French Quarter. While tour guides delight in describing the unsanitary waste-disposal practices of the old Creole days, the stench arising from back alleys is actually more recent in origin.

Public rest rooms can be found in the Jackson Brewery mall, off St Peter St, and in the French Market. Larger hotels often have accessible rest rooms off the lobby, usually near the elevators and pay phones.

TOURIST INFORMATION
Right next to popular Jackson Sq in the heart of the Quarter, the **New Orleans Welcome Center** (Map pp40-1, F3; ☎ 566-5031; 529 St Ann St; ☙ 9am-5pm), in the lower Pontalba Building, offers maps, up-to-date pocket guidebooks, listings of upcoming events and a variety of brochures for sights, restaurants and hotels. The friendly staff can help you find accommodations in a pinch, answer questions and offer advice about New Orleans.

Information kiosks scattered through main tourist areas offer most of the same brochures as the Welcome Center, but their staff tend not to be as knowledgeable.

Information on Louisiana tourism can be obtained through the mail from **Louisiana Office of Tourism** (☎ 342-8119, 800-414-8626; PO Box 94291, Baton Rouge, LA, 70804).

WOMEN TRAVELERS
Intoxicated bands of men in the Quarter and along parade routes are a particular nuisance. Otherwise respectable students and businessmen are transformed by New Orleans. Women in any attire are liable to receive lewd comments. More provocative outfits will lead to a continuous barrage of requests to 'show your tits.' This occurs on any Friday or Saturday night, not just during

DIRECTORY

Mardi Gras. Many men assume that any woman wearing impressive strands of beads has acquired them by displaying herself on the street. Any serious problems you encounter (including assault or rape) should be reported to the **police** (☎ 911). The YWCA offers a **Rape Crisis Hotline** (☎ 483-8888), as

well as a **Battered Women's Hotline** (☎ 486-0377).

The New Orleans branch of **Planned Parenthood** (Map pp88-9, G5; ☎ 897-9200; 4018 Magazine St) provides health-care services for women, including pregnancy testing and birth-control counseling.

>INDEX

See also separate subindexes for See (p167), Shop (p168), Eat (p166), Drink (p166) and Play (p167).

DRINK

000 map pages

EAT